GOLD MEDAL WINNER

PRESIDENT'S BOOK AWARD

FLORIDA AUTHORS AND PUBLISHERS ASSOCIATION

2022

SLUE FOOT

A BLACK GIRL GROWS UP IN MIDWEST AMERICA

A Memoir

MARGARET EDWARDS

SLUE FOOT: A Black Girl Grows Up in Midwest America

Edited by Cortni Merritt
Cover Design, Typography & Production by Hallard Press LLC/John W Prince

Published by Hallard Press LLC.
www.HallardPress.com Info@HallardPress.com 352-234-6099
Bulk copies of this book can be ordered at Info@HallardPress.com

Printed in the United States of America 1

Publisher's Cataloging-in-Publication data

Names: Edwards, Margaret, 1945-, author.
Title: Slue foot : a Black girl grows up in Midwest America / Margaret Edwards.
Description: The Villages, FL: Hallard Press LLC, 2021.
Identifiers: LCCN: 2021902462 | ISBN: 978-1-951188-16-0 (print) | 978-1-951188-18-4 (ebook)
Subjects: LCSH Edwards, Margaret, 1945-. | African American women--Illinois--Biography. | African American women--Middle West--Biography. | United States--Race relations--History--20th century. | Migration, Internal--United States. | African Americans--Migrations--History--20th century. | Rural-urban migration--United States--History--20th century. | BISAC BIOGRAPHY & AUTOBIOGRAPHY / Cultural, Ethnic & Regional / African American & Black | BIOGRAPHY & AUTOBIOGRAPHY / Personal Memoir
Classification: LCC E185.915 .E39 2021 | DDC 977/.0496073/092--dc23

ISBN: 978-1-951188-16-0 (print); 978-1-951188-18-4 (ebook)

Dedication:

To the memory of my mother and father,
and to my sisters and brothers who made my story possible.

Table of Contents

Chapter One

Story Time

"Quit it—t... stop, stop it."

I was almost four years old and scrambling to my feet, trying to escape the tip of that hot poke iron my seven-year-old sister Ruth jabbed at me. My other siblings—Junior (twelve), Mae (eleven), Leeah (nine), and Jean (five)—were sitting on the floor in the front room of our house. They were enjoying the chase . Frank (two) and the baby, Helena, were sleeping.

"Put dat poke iron down, Ruth, an set you butt down."

Daddy grabbed the switch from the side of the fireplace. He swatted Ruth once across her legs but she dodged a second swat. Daddy warned her, "I ain't gon tell you no mo."

We resettled in our places on the floor. It was wintertime in Grenada, Mississippi, and planting season was over for now. In the evenings, we sat in the light and warmth of the fireplace waiting for Mama and Daddy to tell us stories about the old days and waiting for those sweet potatoes roasting in the fireplace to cook.

We sometimes had to go to bed early, because Ruth messed

everything up, but not tonight.

"Mama, tell de one 'bout de haint."

Ruth knows that story is scary. She liked to see me cover my face when Mama said, "Wen I wuz a lit'l girl, a haint would git in bed wit me. I know it wuz Grandma Beck 'cause she jes died. I knowed she got in my bed—the matress would go down. She didn't say nothin. Jes stay awhil den git up an go."

I heard that story so many times before. But still, when I went to bed, I couldn't sleep. I was watching and waiting for that haint to make my mattress go down.

"Daddy, kin you tell us de one 'bout de bird dat took Junior?"

This was my favorite story, because it had a happy ending.

"Well," Daddy began, "a bird or somethin picked up Junior off de road an took him away. He wuz jes two yeahs old. Me, Cora Mae, an de baby wuz walking home on dis dirt road we walk on eveyday. De baby wuz jes learning how ta walk, so he wuz walking real slow ret behin us. But wen we turned 'round, he wuzn't dere. We went back ta de field, walked all thu de grass—no Junior. We wuz looking eveywhere, calling 'Junior—Junior.'

"Den we wuz coming back on de road an dere down de road wuz dat baby walking. We run down dere an we could see three or four footsteps in de dirt, lak somebidy jes set dat baby down. I wuz neva so skared in my life. We still don't know who took dat baby an den brung him back."

I was happy after that story. I could tell eveybody else was, too. Junior was looking around and smiling and sitting a little taller. While we took a sigh of relief that Junior was brought back, Mae raked the cooked sweet potatoes out of the fireplace. She rolled one to each of us. We peeled and ate real slow.

Daddy had one more story to tell about when he was a little boy. We didn't ask him to tell us this one. He liked telling it anyway.

"Der wuz dis big famly jes lak us, but dey wun't po lak us. I seed dem girls in dey pressed white dresses always carrying theirselves lak dey wuz somebody. Der wuz five girls. Dey looked smart, went ta school everyday, an wuz at church evey Sunday. Dey had dey heads up high, an dey wuz real intelligent lookin. Dey got in dey wagons, set up strait behind dey parents, an went home. I never seed dem run 'round wit nobody, 'specially dem 'no-good ' boys. Dey wuz beautiful. When I seed dat, I use ta wish dat wuz my family. I say dats wat I wont my family ta be lak, an dat's wat I wont my chillun ta be lak."

We loved listening to Daddy's story about his "dream family" and his "dream girls" from when he was a little boy. We had heard the story over and over again. But we never thought the five of us girls would be part of that "beautiful" family of his childhood. But we were.

When I look back on my childhood, I grew up in a family with a strict, rules-driven, hard-working father who seemed determined to create his 'dream girls and dream family' despite the changing times around us. Sisterly rebellions, old and young men "playing nasty", trifling relatives and ministers, and racial segregation was the environment of my childhood. To carve out a space for me to thrive, I had to be audacious.

My Daddy, William T. Edwards, was born and raised in Grenada, Mississippi, in a destitute sharecropper family. Unlike his father, who was a "lazy, womanizing , philanderer who was away from home days at a time chasing skirt tails," Daddy was the man of the house at a very young age. In addition to working the fields, he worked in the sawmills, and on the railroads. He wanted to go to school, but his father wanted him to work to make money for the family.

My mother was born Cora Mae Hill in Grenada, Mississippi, but raised in Hawkins, Mississippi, after her father died and her mother re-married. Mama loved her short, good life with her father who farmed and worked for the army. When her sister, Erma (thirteen) and Daddy's brother Lester (fifteen) ran off and got married, Mama welcomed Daddy's courting overtures. They got married in December 1934, four months after Lester and Erma. Mama was fifteen years old; Daddy was nineteen.

Daddy wanted to create a life very different from that of his childhood. By working as sharecroppers, day and night for four years, he and Mama were able to save up enough money to buy a 240-acre farm from the sons of rich White farmers who "just wanted to get rid of it." They became landowners. And for the next seven years, Daddy and Mama worked land that they owned.

But times changed, WWII happened and yet, their hard work persisted. The family grew from one son, to five girls in a row, to two more babies in diapers. It was going to be impossible to maintain the productivity of the farm. From not having enough "hands" to farm, to constant urging from *The Chicago Defender* and from Big Mama, Daddy made the decision to heed the call and leave Mississippi. He followed the throngs of other Colored families migrating north for jobs and better schooling.

Chapter Two

From Mississippi to Big Mama

"Cora Mae, we leaving Mississippi."

"Wat you talkin 'bout, Willie T?" Mama asked.

I was watching, looking, and listening.

Mama switched baby Helena from her left hip to her right. Daddy was on the porch yelling to Mama through the screen door.

"I'se been tryin to sell this place fer two yeahs, and dese peckerwoods wont to give me nothin fer it. I know wen dey cheatin me."

Daddy came in the house. "I work like a damn dog. I gotta git outta dis heah place."

Mama was still asking, "We cain't leav jes like dat—wat 'bout da crops? I thought we wuz goin wait a whil longa."

Daddy started sweeping out the fireplace with a bunch of straw reeds tied together with string. He turned to Mama, "Don't jes keep asting questions. We been waiting all our life fer peckerwoods. We ain't gon wait no mo. I better git outta Mississippi 'fore I kill dem damn bastards. Dis heah is prime property, and all dey wont to give me is wat I paid fer it eight yeahs ago?"

Daddy dumped the ashes into the trash bucket.

"For years, these peckerwoods been cheating us. I ain't goin' keep werking my ass off an giving eveythang ta dem White bastards. White folks do everthan they kin to keep colored folks from doin better than dem."

Mama was staring wide-eyed at Daddy, like she was trying to see inside his head.

"Mama, where we goin to?" Ruth asked.

"Hush, y'all gon' outside," Mama said to Jean, Ruth, and me. I could tell Mama was scared, because she started talking to herself. Her lips were moving in a whispering conversation.

Daddy was still making the case for leaving. "Cora Mae, ain't Mrs. Bertha been talkin 'bout all de jobs up dere in Mt. Vernon? I seen the kind of money I kin make. You seed the money I come home wit from Milwaukee. I made mo money in dem two monts den I made all yeah on dis farm! The Chicago paper say all da time 'bout wat Negroes is doin up dere. Dey say Illinois is gonna free everbidy. I wanna fin me a job where I kin make a livin like a man. I ain't gon let dese White folks 'round heah push me 'round no mo. We leavin heah."

We wouldn't be the first in the family to leave Mississippi and head North. Mama's family started it. Big Mama with Uncle John and Aunt Belle left to follow Cousin Willie Mae, who left two years before. "Up North" for them was Mt. Vernon, Illinois.

Nobody knew anything about Mt. Vernon, except what Big Mama said, "The best schools and jobs everywhere."

Daddy's sisters and brothers, at different times, had drifted north also, to Memphis, St. Louis, and New York. His oldest sister, Helen, got a job in St. Louis and brought Big Papa and Grandmother Ophelia to live with her. Only his sister Ethyl remained in Mississippi.

Daddy piled us into the cab of his old, green Dodge flatbed truck. He covered the back with a tarpaulin. That truck was Daddy's lifeline. He used it to haul crops to sell, to deliver crops to the landlord, and to haul our family. It was big with wide, high fenders. It had mirrors that stuck out on the sides and lots of tall poles sticking up in the back. It had two big lights in the front and smaller ones in the back—so many things to touch, pull, and sit on.

Sometimes, Daddy had to load us all in the truck and drive to the field he was working that day. He parked the truck as close as possible to the field. Jean and I played sometimes near the pallet where the babies were sleeping or crying, and other times we played near the truck. One time Jean and I were playing at the truck jumping on and off the fenders.

Then Jean said, "These lights are like bug eyes. Let's ride 'um into the field."

We each mounted a light and jumped up and down, pumping that "bug" to move faster.

"Gitty up! Gitty up! Go, go!"

Then, I saw Daddy running up the road, breathing hard, his arms in the air yelling, "Get off dem lights. Get offa dere. Y'all wont a whooping?"

He grabbed my arm and pulled me into the dirt. Looking from Jean to me, he threatened, "I should whoop yo ass for settin on dem lights. You know betta dan to break dem lights."

I found out later that we were riding those bug lights so hard, we failed to notice Reverend Tison walk by. I hated that reverend for telling Daddy about such a small thing. That's the way people were in Grenada, somebody was always watching.

* * *

We left Mississippi in March of 1949. Our destination was Mt. Vernon, Illinois, "a city in the country," as described by the Chamber of Commerce. The city had a population of 15,000. About 13,500 were White and less than 1,500 were Colored.

I don't remember much about the packing and the loading of the truck. But I do remember asking Mama: "Where everybidy else at? Is dey coming wit us?"

Mama knew I was talking about Junior, Mae, Leeah, and Ruth.

She answered, "Dey at skool. We gon git dem 'fore we go."

Daddy turned the truck off the main dirt road into what looked like a forest of trees. I was sitting in the cab next to Daddy. All I could see out the window was the brown and green tops of trees. Mama was squeezed in next to me with Frank and Helena in her arms. I heard the tires crushing weeds and saw the windows being slapped by overhanging leaves and branches. I wished Helena would stop crying and go to sleep like Frank so I could hear things better. Daddy was wrestling with the steering wheel. I guess he was trying to keep from hitting things in the road like small trees, mangled bushes, and tree stumps.

We finally reached a clearing. I was able then to lean forward to see a white, wooden structure with long planks leading up to an open door. Standing on the steps was a small man in a dark suit peering over wire spectacles.

"Who's that man?" I asked.

Daddy answered this time, "Dat's de techah, Mr. Hardiman."

At his side were Junior, Mae, Leeah, and Ruth. When they saw the truck, they raced down the steps and climbed onto the back. Daddy climbed down out of the truck and walked up to the man who was wiping his eyes. Daddy shook his hand for a long time.

We waved to the man standing alone on the steps as our truck made its way back into the forest of small trees, mangled bushes, and tree stumps.

* * *

The first things I saw when I woke up somewhere on the road, were lights and cars. Houses were all lit up, and lights were up on poles and on porches. Cars were going by with the faces of White people flashing by in open windows. Colored men and women were walking, some of them walking real fast, with bags busting at the seams full of stuff. Some were all dressed up in Sunday clothes, and it wasn't even Sunday.

Daddy brought the truck to a stop in front of a small, white house surrounded by tall grass and a low picket fence. He banged on the back window of the truck, "Wake up, y'all. We heah."

I saw a woman's Black face near the window on Daddy's side of the truck. She was talking to him, "How you, T? Glad y'all made it—Come on this side. Turn in the driveway."

One by one, the back of the truck emptied out Jean, Leeah, Ruth, Mae, and Junior. I was climbing to the ground from the cab by myself.

This must be Big Mama.

I knew her name, but I thought she was going to look like Mama—tall and light skinned with good hair and a big belly. This Big Mama was nothing like Mama. Her skin was dark, like she could be Daddy's mama, and she was short and round all over, not just in the front like Mama. She had on a flowered pink dress, brown stockings with a knot below her knees, and pink shoes on her feet. And her hair was 'done'.

She was shaking hands with Daddy and hugging Mama now. She took baby Helena into her arms. "I'm so glad to see y'all," Big Mama was holding onto a struggling, whining Helena and talking and laughing at the same time. "Look at you kids, so big and healthy. Junior, you so tall, and Mae—look at that hair, you shor got a head of hair on you—and is this Leeah? Girl, you look just like your mama."

She crossed the front patch of grass, gathering up Jean and Ruth. I was wrapped in Mama's dress skirt and not available for gathering. She led us to a small sagging porch with two gray wooden swings on each end of the porch. They were hanging with chains, like the ones at our house in Mississippi.

Big Mama was pulling open a screen door. "Come on in. Y'all have a seat."

We each squeezed through a tiny door, trying not to stumble over each other. It was so dark. Lights everywhere outside, but no lights in here. When my eyes adjust, I see that the two windows were covered with brown curtains. We were standing in a small room with a lot of brown stuff, a couch and two chairs. There was one blue chair. The backs and seats of the couch and chairs were layered with sheets and blankets. Small pink and blue pillows were on the corners of the couch and the chairs.

I looked around, but I kept holding onto Mama's skirt. The two side tables had stiff pink doilies circling the two lamps in the room. We were just standing in the middle of the room, waiting, and looking.

Daddy sat down in the blue chair, pulling Frank onto his lap. Mama sat down on the couch with Helena on her lap. I squeezed in next to her. Everybody else went outside to the swings.

Big Mama must have been cooking all day. I know the smell of collards and fried chicken and cake. All that smelled so good, but I wanted some cornbread and buttermilk. I wanted to crumble up a big piece of cornbread and then pour a glass full of buttermilk on top and mix it all together. When that cornbread was all wet, I wanted to go to a quiet corner and put big spoonfuls into my mouth and chew real slow with my eyes closed. When you want to eat cornbread and buttermilk though, you have to be real careful.

I remember going up the hill to Aunt Erma's house in Grenada, and she handed me a glass of buttermilk mixed with bread. I was headed to a quiet place when I put a big spoonful in my mouth. I chewed one time, and my mouth knew something was wrong. The buttermilk was mixed with biscuit! Biscuit!? *Where was the cornbread?*

I just stood there like a statue, my mouth open wide. Buttermilk biscuit was dripping down my chin, down my dress, and in-between my bare toes. I had to do something. I could close my mouth, swallow and be sick, or I could keep my mouth open and drip my way down the hill and home. I dripped home.

There were no cows in Big Mama's yard, so I thought, *Big*

Mama must not have any buttermilk. I saw cornstalks on the side of the house, so I figured she probably had some cornbread.

Chapter Three

The Little Yellow House

Big Mama's house was real crowded with so many of us sleeping everywhere. Mama, Helena, Frank, and me slept in Big Mama's big lumpy bed. Daddy and Junior slept on the back of the truck. Everybody else slept on the floor on pallets made up from all those quilts and blankets from the couch and chairs.

Daddy was acting like he was in a hurry to get out of Big Mama's house. He doesn't even unload the truck. He came into the house, ate a piece of bread with butter, and then went outside to tinker with the truck. By midmorning, he and Junior were gone. He never told us where he was going. After about three days of going in the truck, he finally came in the house, smiled and stayed awhile. He said: "We movin to our own house."

"Our own house" turned out to be an off-the-road, small, wood-frame yellow house with the paint peeling off and rotting planks for siding. It was on 27th Street about a walking mile from Big Mama's house. It had three rooms. Each room had a window and a hanging light bulb. There was no kitchen and no stove. I guess it was a summer house. There was a waterlogged double-sided wooden picnic table out front in the grass bare courtyard with a firepit next to it.

Daddy always said Colored folks had to be on guard when dealing with White folks. He also said Colored folks had to be on guard when dealing with Colored folks, too. A Colored man named Mr. Stetson owned the little yellow house. He also owned two other houses on the main road. He lived in one. I never saw Mr. Stetson, but Mrs. Fannie, the Colored lady who lived across the creek on 28th Street, called him "an uppity Negro."

I was scared to look at Mr. Stetson's house. I know it was big and white with green side shutters. The windows and curtains were always closed, and nobody ever was on the wraparound porch. If a Colored man lived there, he sure did act White. Maybe that was because he was the only Colored man living on 27th Street.

His other house was on the main road and in front of the yellow house we lived in. It was just like the one Mr. Stetson lived in— big, white, wide wraparound porch, and tall windows. We could see that no one lived there.

So, Mama said: "Dat's good. We kin cook up dere."

Mr. Stetson must have known what Mama was thinking. The next day, he sent her a piece of paper with some rules on it:

Mama could go up to that empty house to use the kitchen **only** when it was raining. There were other rules like:

- Only enter the kitchen through the back door.
- Only use the stovetop—never use the oven.
- Only use your assigned shelf in the refrigerator.
- Only adults allowed in the house—never children.

Daddy just said: "Wat did I say 'bout Colored folks? We gotta git outta dis place 'fore winter sets in."

I hoped it would rain everyday. Then Mama could use the stove and make some hotcakes, beans, cabbage, and fried chicken. Sometimes when it rained, she would make a lot of food so we could have it for a few days. We needed another shelf in the refrigerator, too, but Mama was afraid to ask for one.

Sundays was always the best, because we would go to Big Mama's house. She knew we were coming, so she had all kinds of food: chicken, ribs, potato salad, greens and cakes. Always cakes. What we couldn't eat, we would bring back home to our yellow house and eat it the next day.

Daddy kept saying: "We's gotta git out of dis place 'fore it gits cold."

"Sho do," Mama said. "We may hav ta move back ta Mama's house."

Daddy said: "We ain't goin back dere."

Mama was quiet then.

He always said: "I'se my own man, an I don't wont nothin from nobidy."

Mama reminded him: "Ain't nothin wrong wit dat, but we don't know nobidy up heah 'cept Mama an Mae Liza. And wat we gon do witout dem givin us stuff or telling us where ta git it?"

That little house had some stuff in it, like two straight-back wooden chairs and a sagging blue couch. Daddy got some cots and some dishes from the Rescue Mission.

We at least had a roof over our heads, but it was hot under that roof and in the courtyard. And the mosquitoes were biting.

* * *

Now that we had a house, Daddy had to get everybody in school.

According to Big Mama, "The only school in town fer Colored kids is Booker T. Washington School, a fine school. The other school fer Mae and Junior is Casey Jr. High School. It ain't no Colored school. Everybidy go to school together over there. Belle and John went to that school, an to the high school, too. Everybody is real nice in them schools."

I didn't go to sign-up for school, because I wasn't six yet.

When everybody got home from school, Jean was the happiest. "I'm in first grade, and I was talking to my teacher. Her name is Miss Low, and she is real pretty and nice."

Ruth was put in third grade and Leeah in fifth grade. They reported the experience to be "Okay."

Daddy, Mae and Junior were real mad. Daddy said, "We went ta dat junior high school, but dis ole White principal didn't pit Mae an Junior in dey rite grade. Dey say we didn't hav no papers. I told dat peckerwood, 'I ain't got no papers, an you better pit my kids in skool.' So, dey pit Mae in sixth grade at Washington School an Junior in seventh grade in junior high skool."

Mae didn't say anything. Junior already said he needs new clothes if he was "going to be in school with Colored kids and White kids. And them White teachers probably gon ask me something I don't know."

* * *

I liked eating outside at the picnic table. There were no lights out there, so Mama usually built a little fire in the dugout pit to keep the mosquitoes away. And sometimes, we brought out our kerosene lanterns.

At every meal, Daddy put out a loaf of Wonder bread, a jar of mayonnaise, and a big roll of bologna or sliced hoghead cheese. Mae sliced the bologna. Sometimes we cut open a watermelon. On really good days, we had food from Big Mama's or from our leftover shelf in the refrigerator. And on even better days, Daddy and Mama would tell stories after we finished eating.

Leeah asked, "Can you tell us about when you and Mama wuz real poor kids in Mississippi?"

Daddy took the cue. "Everybidy in Mississippi wuz po, 'specially Colored folks. We didn't have nothin. We wuz livin in de backwoods with one mule and a wagon. We wuz always moving from one sharecropper place to anotha."

"Why y'all move so much?" Leeah wanted to know.

"We had ta move. We wuz livin in a sharecropper house. If we didn't pick 'nough cotton an grow a lotta crops, some of dem landlords jes tell us ta leav. Sometimes, dey would take all de crop, dey half an our half. Den dey lock de barn an we had ta leav walkin or ridin wit nowher ta live."

"Mama, were y'all poor like Daddy?"

"No, No. Wen I wuz little, we wuz livin real good. We had a nice place an my daddy wuz makin good money. But wen he died, eveythang wuz a mess. I wuz seven yeahs old. Mama married a ol man name Big Boy. An we moved ta his house in Hawkins, Mississippi. I hated it up dere. He say he had money. He didn't have nothin, an he didn't know a thang 'bout farming an bout raising no kids. We wuz begging Mama ta take us back ta Dubars place. We stayed up dere wit Big Boy fer almost seven yeahs 'fore we moved back. When Erma run off and married Lester, that's wen Willie and me started talking and got married."

Daddy adds, "Wen me an Cora Mae wuz married, I made a vow at dat time dat I would do all de work an take care of my family. It wuz my job ta make a living, ta pay de bills, do de farm work, an make a fine house. Cora Mae's job wuz ta stay home, take care of de house an de kids. De kids wuz jes ta go ta skool."

"Mama, you wanted to stay at home all the time an take care of kids?" Mae asked.

Daddy answered for Mama. "Cora Mae knowed wat I wonted. She knowed I didn't wont her ta werk. De home come 'fore anythang else."

Mama didn't say anything. I guessed she agreed with Daddy.

One day after about a month of living in that little yellow house, and when everybody was sitting around the picnic table, Daddy started to speak: "I bought some land ta build a house." He was biting down on a piece of corn from our shelf in the refrigerator.

"Wat chu say Willie T?" Mama asked.

Leeah interpreted, "He said he got some land and a house."

"Wat?—We gotta house?—Where it at?—Kin we see it?"

Everybody who could talk was talking all at once.

"Y'all stop makin all dat nois. You wont Mr. Stetson ta come out heah?" Mama said.

Daddy sucked on his front teeth to remove pieces of corn: "Jes be quiet."

He waited. We waited.

"De land is on 28th Street, ret over dere 'cross the creek from Fannie May. It ain't in de city, like heah on 27th Street. We don't git things lak lights on de road, an water from no fusset. We don't need dem thangs. We didn't have all dat stuff in Mississippi an we don't need it now. I'se gonna build a shed first, an its a big pesa land, 'bout five acres."

"We gon live in a shed?"

"We ain't gon' live in no shed. I gon' build a house."

"You gon build the house by yourself?"

"You damn right I gon build de house by myself. Who you thank built yo house in Mississippi? Dat farm had two houses on it, and I built another one by myself. I built dat house. Don't tell me nothin' 'bout building no house."

* * *

In Mississippi, everybody was your friend and neighbor and they were expected to show up to offer a hand or to just sit around, watch and talk. So, when we were building our house on 28th Street, we expected the neighbors to come by to see what was going on and talk.

"How y'all doin? Y'all must not be from 'round here. Y'all need something, we jes ret down the road."

28th Street was not a long street. At one end was a dirt crossroad called Fisher's Lane. At the other end and down the hill was Circle Drive. The baseball field and the city park were on Circle Drive. There were five families on 28th Street, three Colored and two White.

The McDonald family was White and lived on the hill that

led down to the baseball field. They had a daughter in third grade named Karen.They just said "Hello" and kept to themselves.

Another White family, Ed and Peggy Hines had four kids, two stringy-haired girls, Carol and Kay in junior high, and two burly older boys, Earl and Roy who didn't go to school. They lived two cornfields away from the McDonalds in one direction, and two cornfields and a wagon path from our house in the other direction. Daddy called them "po White trash" because of the cars, bicycles, and motorcycles in various stages of repair parked all over their yard. The girls came out sometimes to look at our house and talk. The boys were always tinkering with their old cars and motorcycles and occasionally racing them down past our house in clouds of dirt and dust.

Across the street from our house was a "nosy" Colored woman named Miss Fannie. The creek and the plank bridge to 27th Street were behind her house. She was a longtime resident of 28th Street and was always ready to talk about everything and everybody.

All the way down at the end of the road on the corner of 28th and Fishers Lane lived a Colored couple, Little Moe and his wife, Mrs. Tiny. They had a store in the front room of their clapboard house. They didn't sell much, just hard candy, white bread, bologna, and sour pickles. Little Joe was short and squat, and Mama said he was blind in one eye. Mrs. Tiny was "tiny" and was always sitting in a rocking chair outside in the small, grass bare yard drinking soda pop, laughing with visitors and swatting flies.

Mr. and Mrs. Tarnes didn't live on 28th Street. They were a Colored couple who lived up the hill in the field between our house and the Hines' house. Mr. Tarnes was tall and thin and Mrs. Tarnes was round and fat. Ruth called them "Fatty and Skinny."

We were always trying to figure out how both of them fit into the same bed in that little one-room house.

Every time we walked by going to the pigpen or to pick plums, they would be sitting in their yard under the shade of the old oak tree.

They would wave. "How you chillun doin taday?"

We would wave back. "Fine."

We were hoping our friendly smiles disguised Ruth's whisperings of "Fatty and Skinny was in the bed..."

Plus, we were always wondering where their son Alfie slept when he came to visit. Ruth said Alfie was a "sissy," 'cause he was always talking, strutting, waving his hands and playing the piano like a TV movie star. We liked him anyway, but we still never figured out where he slept.

Chapter Four

House to Home

The house building began in April of 1949. Every morning, Daddy was up early.

"Mae, Ruth—y'all get up an git ready fer school. Y'all wont a ride, ya better git in de truck now."

For the next two months, I spent most of my time with Daddy, house building. Sometimes Mama told me to feed Helena some mashed up cornbread with butter in it. I didn't mind feeding her, because I picked out the crusty pieces of bread and ate those myself. I kept thinking how much better it would be though if I had some buttermilk to go with that crusty bread.

On days that Daddy didn't drive everybody to school, he would say to me, "Margaret, we goin ta de lumba yard."

These were my best days. I climbed into the cab of the truck, sitting as close as I could to the front window so I could see everything. I saw concrete footpaths along the side of roads and tall buildings with lots of windows. I saw White people walking, sitting on porches, and going in and out of stores. I saw White kids running and laughing on their way to school. I saw tall trees and bushes in front of houses, but not much dirt. I didn't see any Colored folks on our way to the lumberyard.

When we get there, a White man with a hammer hooked to his overalls stops us and asks, "Kin I help y'all?

Daddy reads from a piece of paper: "I need ten 2x4s, eight 2x6s, thirty red bricks, and six sheets of drywall."

Back on 28th Street, I helped unload the truck, one brick at a time. Sometimes Daddy quizzed me about building stuff.

"Where is the 2x4's?"

"Here."

"What's this called?"

"Drywall."

Sometimes, he asked me to name the tools he had in the yard, like, "Where's de trowl, de level, de horse?"

Every time I got them right. He just laughed. "You got dat right. Now you kin help me make de plaster."

I was Daddy's helper. He measured and mixed the powder and water with a hoe in a big long metal tub. My job was to keep pushing the hoe back and forth in that mixture to keep it soft for laying the bricks. When I wasn't doing that, I picked up rocks, leaves, and twigs that were in his way. Best of all, it was just my Daddy and me working together, laying the foundation for our new house.

Every weekend and when school was out in May, the whole family got up early, crossed the creek, and helped with the building. Daddy was directing. We were leveling, sawing, hammering, and stirring. Mama didn't help with stuff cause her stomach was too big. When she walked across the creek to the house, she just sat down on a horse, which was a wooden triangle shaped bench used to hold lumber for sawing.

Sometimes Daddy slept in the shed he built. He wanted to be up early in the morning so he could keep working. We didn't see him much on 27th Street, except at suppertime in the courtyard.

Mae and Leeah sometimes walked Jean and me up to see the house in the evening. We couldn't go alone, because we had to cross the creek that had a bridge made of wobbly wooden planks. The creek was not deep, and most of the time had no water in it but Mama had her rule.

Every time we saw the house, there was something new. In the backyard, a henhouse was attached to the back of the shed, and another little house was added across the yard that Daddy called "a smokehouse." In the grassy areas behind the shed, there was a white picket fence all around the yard. It had a gate in front by the henhouse.

Sunday was our day to go to Big Mama's house, mostly to get some good food. But if Daddy was too busy working on the house, Big Mama walked to our house on 27th Street after church. She dropped off a basket of food and crossed the creek to 28th Street.

* * *

When our house was almost finished, Colored folks from town started coming by walking real slow and sometimes driving in old beat-up cars. They say they were on their way to the park. That didn't matter, because they would stop and talk.

"How y'all doin' dis ev'nin'? Fine place y'all got there."

Big Mama said, "I knows why so many people is coming by

heah. You see, these heah Colored folks—and some White folks, too—they don't understand how a Colored man from Mississippi can do somthin like this. You come up here to Mt. Vernon, buy land, and build this kind of house! They just want to know how's this possible. And wit all these kids. Hee, hee. They say, 'Who is this Colored man? Where he from? Where he get money to build a house like this? I just laugh and I say, 'Dat's my son-in-law, Willie T—he's a fine man, a good worker."

Mama told us one time that Big Mama may like Daddy now, but she didn't want her to marry him at first.

"Your Big Mama said, 'Willie T is too dark, didn't go to school, an he's gonna be jes lak his lazy, no-good Daddy.' She laked Johnny B, my other friend, cause he wuz real smart an finished tenth grade. An he wuz a good-lookin boy—real light, wit curly hair. He wuz always talkin an sayin werds in Franch. He say it wuz de way folks talked in France. He wuz real edgicated. I laked dem bofe. But I didn't lak de name 'Willie.' I thank his name should be jes Will—well, I laked Willie better. So, Mama stopped saying bad thangs about him."

I knew we would be moving into our house soon when I saw two White men with a big machine dig a hole on the side of the house by the garden and dig another hole in the back of the fenced in yard.

I asked Daddy, "Wat dey digging fer?"

He said: "Dis one is a well fer drinking wata. Dat one back dere is de toilet."

I was there another time and saw a Colored man with a mule pulling a plow in the grassy area on the other side of the well. Daddy said: "He turning over the soil fer planting a garden."

* * *

In September, just before the cold weather set in, we left that three-room little house on 27th Street. We would no longer be down the hill, off the main road and hidden from life. Our family of eleven moved into a new six-room house built by Daddy and me, with some help from the rest of the family.

This was the prettiest house I ever saw. And according to Daddy: "Dis house got everthan it suppose to have—a big pictha winda, a girage, a white picket fence, and a piana."

The house was built the way he wanted it to be built. That was one of his jobs.

The front had two brick pillars on each side of the concrete sidewalk that connected the road to the house. It had three wide steps to get to the concrete porch that ran from one side of the house to the other. The porch was painted a dark red color, just like the window shutters. Two tall square white columns were placed at each end of the porch and two more were at the top of the steps. In front of the house next to the front door was that "big pictha winda."

There were three bedrooms, one on each side of the front room, and one next to the dining room. The left front bedroom had green wallpaper. The right front bedroom had pink-and-white striped wallpaper. The one by the dining room had blue wallpaper.

Everything in the living room was new, the green flowery couch, a fancy white mirror with little shelves inside, a brown cabinet with a radio and record player in it, and a big brown upright piano. The kitchen, pantry, and bathroom were on the other side of the dining room.

To get to the dining room from the living room, there was a rounded archway with shelves for pictures and vases. In the middle of the dining room was a long brown table with six matching chairs with green cushions. The back door to go outside was behind the table. In the center of the room was a black, potbelly stove with a flat top for pots and a teakettle.

Daddy said: "In de winter, dis stove is all we need ta heat de whole house."

A tin bucket of coals waited behind the stove. To the left of the dining room was the all-white kitchen. There is an oil cooking stove with dangling handles, a sink, a metal table, and two plastic-covered chairs. Next to the kitchen was the bathroom. In there was a long table with a folded towel, a tin wash pan, and a slop jar.

The garage was attached to the right side of the house. We didn't have a car, and the truck was too big to fit in there. For the time being, it bcame a storage shed for all the leftover building stuff.

* * *

Our house was sitting back from the road and I could see all that white, red and green. It was like a picture I saw once in a magazine—everything new and pretty like nobody lived there. We moved in there, and to keep the house looking like a magazine picture, Daddy made some rules.

"You kain't play in de front yard. You kain't set on de front porch. Wen you play outside, you kin only play in de backyard. You kain't sit in de living room. You kin go in dere if you gon play de piana."

There were also some other rules that I learned. There were words we could use and words we were not allowed to use. To call somebody a really bad name, we could use any animal name like, "you buzzard, you weasel, you cow, or you skunk". When talking about White folks, we could use words from the animal list, and other words like, "peckerwood, White trash, goofy, and flat-behind."

We couldn't say "bad words". We could say "poop, doodoo, your booty, or your between-the-legs." We could never say words like "butt, hell, or damn."

There were no "word" rules for Daddy. Words like "damn, ass, and hell" were sprinkled throughout his everyday conversation. When he was angry, anybody Colored or White, was a "son-of-a-bitch, a bastard, or a liar." He used all these words and more, **except on Sundays.**

I didn't care about these rules. My sisters didn't either. We just wanted to play up and down the hills and on the dirt roads.

When we were in Mississippi, Ruth, Jean, and I were always outside running and climbing over our barbed wire fence, and trying to get away from wasps. We held stalks of sorghum that they wanted. Those wasps chased us all the way home. Sometimes, they missed the sorghum, caught me, and they stung my eyelid. Mama bathed my swollen eye with baking soda and water to bring down the swelling.

I remember declaring, "I'm ok now," and begging to join my sisters again for the chase.

I remember taking my turn to curl up in a tire inner tube, be pushed down the dirt road in front of our house and spilled out, to yells of approval from my sisters.

I remember the hourly spats between Ruth down the hill, and Cousin Louise up the hill. They called out their mantra to each other from the swing on our front porch and from the steps of her porch: "I ain't gon neeeever play with Louise no mo." And in return, "I ain't gon neeeever play with ole Ruth no mo."

I remember us all playing again a few minutes later.

In Mississippi, I remember never having any rules about where to play.

Chapter Five

Backyard Life

Our backyard was my favorite place around our new house. There was lots of dirt for making mud pies and little mud people. The icebox was next to the back door. Every week the iceman put a big block of ice in the freezer with giant metal clips. Sometimes he picked off pieces of ice for us to sip on. The smokehouse was there, and sometimes it was a very scary place. It was full of all kinds of pig stuff like tails, heads, legs, snouts, and feet hanging from the ceiling on hooks.

We had chickens, too—ten or twelve of them, plus a rooster named Redtop.

According to Daddy, Mama was in charge of the backyard. In Mississippi, Mama was never in charge of nothing. All she did was hoe crops, pick crops, and have babies every year. Now she was telling everybody what to do around the house and in the backyard.

When she got tired of cooking chicken all the time for supper, she would say to Daddy, "I shor wont a rabbit fer supper on Sunday."

Daddy would grab that old shotgun off the top of the cabinet in the dining room, go out to the tool shed, look in the drawer for bullets, and load up. He would go out looking in the tall grass in the back and on the side of the house next to the Hines and bring home one or two rabbits for Mama to skin. It was like he was still in Mississippi, until Ed Hines told him he had to "stop dat shooting 'round heah."

Mama would say: "Jean, go fin some kindling so we kin start a fire. Leeah, go rinse dem dirty dipers off and soak 'em in dis heah bucket."

There was a dugout fire pit in the middle of the yard with a big black kettle sitting on concrete blocks.

"Mae, make shor dere is hot water in dat kettle."

Mama's job was to sit over that tin tub and scrub clothes on the washboard with lye soap she made herself. Ruth, and Jean's, job was to rinse the clothes Mama washed, squeeze them out, and hang them on the two long clotheslines inside the white picket fence.

My job mostly was to "get out of the way" or "hand me a clothes pin."

* * *

The backyard could also be a very dangerous place.

When anybody did something bad, that was where most of the whoopings took place. If one of my sisters did something like hit Frank or Helena or break a toy, Mama or Daddy would say, "Go get a switch, so I can whoop yo ass."

We all knew what kind of switch to get. The best kind was a real thin, long, reed-like piece of tree branch that would sting when you got hit. I never had to get a switch, but I knew the game. The game was to look and look for a long time and come back with a thick branch from a tree.

When asked: "Where dat switch at?"

The answer was always: "I couldn't find no skinny switch, so this is all I could find." Hopefully, the tree branch would be declared "too thick," and hopefully, the reason a switch was needed in the first place was forgotten. Sometimes, the game worked. When it didn't, Daddy could always get the backup switch that was in the dining room behind the potbelly stove.

Ruth was always getting whoopings. Daddy said Ruth was "hardheaded" and "devilish." Daddy would tell her to get a bucket of water from the well, and she wouldn't move. Daddy would tell her again. She still wouldn't move.

Then, he yelled at her: "Ruth, didn't I tell you ta go git some wata? Give me dat switch. You too damn hardheaded."

Ruth slowly moved to the bucket, took her time walking to the door while talking back about why she had to go out. Most of the time, Daddy got tired of telling her things three or four times. He just grabbed the switch from behind the stove, grabbed her arm, and started whooping her.

Ruth had a "bad attitude" too. She pouted, hit, yelled, and broke our toys. And she didn't seem to care that she was going to get a whooping. Sometimes, she got a whooping two or three times a week.

Even Mama had trouble with Ruth. Mama would say, "Come feed de baby."

Ruth just went outside, like Mama wasn't even talking to her. Mama then called her and stood in the door with the switch. Ruth came in through the other door and started feeding the baby.

* * *

"Okay, y'all. Come git yo medicine."

These were words I dreaded. I hated this stuff. Mama called this "sprang cleaning so y'all don't be gitting sick."

Every year in Mississippi, Mama made us line up and choose our medicine, a dose of caster oil or a mixture of Black Draught and sorghum molasses.

I opened my mouth wide for my two teaspoons of caster oil. About an hour later, I would be running fast to find a spot to hide among the trees and bushes to relieve myself. I couldn't see my siblings, but I could hear them running past me to get to higher ground.

But on 28th Street, we were all on guard. We were not in Mississippi anymore. Jean asked: "When I have to doodoo, where I'm going to do that? There ain't nowhere to go and hide. Ain't nothing 'round here but grass."

"Yeah, too many people round here and no trees," Ruth added.

Mama was undeterred.

"Come on over heah an take dis medicine. Dere's plenty places ta go."

The "plenty places" turned out to be between the corn stalks and in the bushes up the hill near the pigpen. Mama was not happy about our chosen destinations, especially when she stepped in our doodoo piles while walking among the corn stalks looking for corn to harvest.

"Sprang cleaning" was a piece of Mississippi life that was abandoned after year one in Mt. Vernon.

* * *

I was a counry farm girl, born into a farming family and yet, I was very suspicious, and sometimes scared, of our farm animals.

We had a brown and white cow named Lucy. She was big and was always eating grass up the hill in the grassy area behind the outdoor toilet. Two or three times a week, Mama would get a bucket and announce, "I'm gon ta milk Lucy."

Mae, Jean, and I would sometimes go to watch, at a distance. Mama would squat down next to Lucy, reach for a tit that looked like it was about to bust wide open, and squeeze it 'til it was empty. She didn't look scared. The whole time, Lucy kept on pulling and chewing grass. Mama kept on squeezing and filling the bucket with milk.

One time she said, "Mae, you need ta learn how ta milk dis heah cow. Come on over heah."

Jean and me inched back, watching Mae squint her eyes and slowly put one bare foot in front of the other, keeping her eyes on Lucy. She bent down next to Mama. Mama stopped squeezing.

"Go on now. Lucy ain't gon do nuting ta you."

Lucy stopped pulling grass. I stopped breathing. Mama pulled Mae's hand and squeezed her fingers around a fat tit. Mae had her head turned back to us, eyes closed. Milk squirted into the bucket. Lucy started pulling grass again. Mae opened her eyes, smiled, and looked at us. I started to breathe again. Another lesson learned on the farm.

If I had a job related to Lucy, it was to take my turn churning milk to make butter, cream, buttermilk, and other stuff. I stood over that clay pot and plunged the wooden paddle into the milk until Mama said, "That's enuff."

Then one day out of nowhere, Daddy said, "Margaret, go git Lucy from up de hill an brang her down heah ta de tool shed."

"I don't know how to git no cow and bring her anywhere. I'm scared of that cow. What if she pulls me and—?"

Daddy walked away.

"Dere ain't nobidy else ta do it. Now go git her 'fore dark."

Cows are big. That cow was big and she didn't look at me. She just kept her head down or looked past me. Cows don't focus. What I needed Lucy to do was to look at me. I had to figure out what she was thinking about doing. Was she going to just walk quietly or was she going to start running and run over me?

I looked at her face for a long time, hoping for a sign. I got nothing. I got the end of her rope, and—keeping my eyes on her every move—I walked slowly down the hill, keeping as far away from her as possible. If she came after me, I wanted to make sure I would have enough time to drop that rope and run.

* * *

We had pigs, too. There was nothing to be afraid of about them, because they were fenced in. But if that fence broke open and those pigs came running after me, I had picked out the tree I was going to climb.

Our pigpen was up the hill near the plum and walnut trees. We had one great big hog, three sows, and about seven or eight baby pigs. I loved going up there and watching those little dirty pink babies try to hang on to the mother's titties. The mother pig was always moving and oinking like she was trying to get away from her dirty little rascals. The little pigs were falling and slipping in mud and in their own doodoo.

Winters or summers after supper, I would go to help take the buckets of slop up to feed the pigs. I could hear the oinking and slouching of mud before we even got there. I loved the smell of pig doodoo mixed with the sweet fragrance of honeysuckles and wildflowers that surrounded the pen. Whatever we had for supper and threw in the garbage bucket—beans, bread, tomatoes, chicken bones, and watermelon rinds—the pigs got it poured into their wooden feeding troughs.

They also got a few ears of dried corn. My favorite sound was the crunching of the dried corn. I was in hog heaven listening to the tearing, the crushing and the grating of the kernels being ripped off the cob. Pigs have no shame. They eat with their mouths wide open, and they don't mind that slop is all over their faces and dripping down their fat jowls.

I would hang over the wooden fence, breathing deeply, watching the sun setting and enjoying the smells and the sounds of crunching and grinding.

* * *

For me, though, the greatest threat in the backyard was our rooster, Redtop.

When Mama said, "Go git dem eggs from de hen house," nobody moved.

Who was she talking to? I know she's not talking to me, because I never have to do anything. But then, I hear my name.

"Margaret, go git dem eggs."

"Who me?" I asked. "I can't reach no eggs. They too high."

"Jes git up on de stool."

I really couldn't go out in that yard and make it to the hen house without getting attacked. I had told Mama and everybody that Redtop was crazy and attacked me every time I went out there by myself.

"You crazy," Ruth said. "You just don't want to go out in the cold."

I was thinking that maybe Redtop felt he had to protect the chickens, because so many of them end up on the table for Sunday dinner. But why did he come after me? Mama was the one who was wringing their necks, that is, until Ruth said she wanted that job.

Chicken neck-wringing time would bring all of us out to the backyard to watch. The chickens, including Redtop, would scatter, clucking their brown and white selves into a frenzy and running around like they knew what was coming. Ruth would be laughing and chasing here and there, grabbing at chickens with one hand, then the other. I was just trying to get out of the way.

Ruth would finally fall on a chicken. "I got one," she would announce holding down a clucking, fluttering bird.

From my hiding place on the back porch, I would let out a breath real slow. Ruth would come up to her feet, chicken in hand.

"Here goes."

She would place the fingers of her right hand tightly around the chicken's neck. Then she would let go of the chicken's body. She would plant her bare feet firmly in the dirt, squeeze her eyes shut, and then begin sharp, short jerks of the chicken's neck. Her arm would be going up and down, up and down. The chickens on the ground would continue muted clucking and scattering, happy that they escaped this time.

The chicken in Ruth's grasp would flutter, trying to protest. Ruth would continue jerking until the chicken seemed to give up and accept her fate. Ruth would then fling the chicken to the ground. The game of "tag" began.

The dying chicken, on unstable feet, ran wildly in circles, then toward the porch, then over to the tool shed. Its neck was dangling to one side and blood was squirting from its protruding, exposed neck bone. Ruth, Jean, and sometimes Leeah would run in all directions, squealing and dodging, trying not to get "tagged." The dying chicken finally stopped, fluttered and shimmied into the dirt—still. Game over.

So, I was thinking that Redtop was already mad. If I had to go out to that henhouse, I needed a way to get there and get those eggs without running into him.

It was cold outside. I decided to put on body protection—my coat, galoshes, a hat, gloves—and to find a stick, just in case. I look like a knight in armor ready for battle.

My battle plan was to surprise Redtop by coming around the side of the house near the garage, instead of going to the yard directly from the back porch. That way, I would have a clear view of the yard and be able to see who was where. If needed, I could run into the tool shed on the right. I approached the battle site by sliding along the wall of the house across from the tool shed, keeping low and looking in every direction.

No Redtop, just clucking hens. All clear.

I moved past the tool shed into the open yard. I stopped and surveyed. My plan was working. I headed across the yard toward the hen house. That's when I heard those hens start sounding like Ruth was chasing them for Sunday dinner. I turned around, and there was Redtop, head down, cocked to the side. He headed in my direction.

I moved strategically toward the hen house. Redtop was trying to follow me, but his sideways-leaning head was causing him to stumble. His body moved toward me, but his head took him to the right of me. His eyes were like Lucy's; he was looking past me. His wings were fluttering up and down, as he lifted himself into short stints of flight. I was pinned between the picket fence gate and the open door to the hen house.

I had to think fast. I had a crazy rooster with a half-screwed-on head jumping, fluttering, clucking and clattering, and coming at me, sort of. I was padded down with coats, boots, and a spear.

Do I fight or do I retreat?

When I got back in the house. Mama said, "Where dem eggs at?"

"Eggs?" I said: "I didn't see no eggs out there."

* * *

The one animal I am glad we didn't have in our backyard was a dog. I had good reason not to trust dogs, or maybe I had good reason not to trust White people with dogs.

One of Mama's White neighbors in Mississippi was Miss Evans, who bought eggs from us. Mama always met her down the dirt road from our house.

One time, Mama and me were walking down that road under the mid-afternoon sun with dust blowing in our faces to sell Miss Evans the usual dozen eggs. Mama was holding a straw-lined box with the twelve eggs that was going get us some money. We were walking real slow so not to jostle those eggs.

We were both barefoot with faded blue head scarves tied under our chins. That dust felt good squishing between my toes. I was carrying nothing, just holding a handful of Mama's sack dress and being dragged along to sell those eggs to Miss Evans. I can't remember what Miss Evans looked like. That was the way it was with White folks in Mississippi; you never looked them in the face.

I heard Mama say, "Evening, Miss Evans".

I saw Miss Evans wearing a straw hat with a white ribbon tied under her chin, walking toward us with her son, BBoy, and his dog, Badger.

She responded, "Evening, Cora."

I was watching BBoy watching me hiding behind Mama's dress. I was thinking, *Why is this big ole boy down here with his mama at a egg-selling meeting?* He ain't never been here before. He is Junior's hunting friend. I was keeping my eyes too on ole, yeller Badger.

While I'm watching from behind Mama's dress tail, BBoy let that dog get away, and he headed straight at me.

I started running 'round Mama's skirt screaming, "Oou, oow."

Mama was yelling to me, "Stop runnin, Margaret. Stan still."

She was trying to get between Badger and me—and hold onto those eggs.

Miss Evans was flinging her wrinkled arms here and there, trying to grab the dog's rope, saying, "Now, Badger, don't do that—come here".

Too late. Badger sank his teeth into my ankle. I was screaming and crying, grabbing my ankle and trying to climb onto Mama's chest. The eggs splattered into the dirt. BBoy was slapping his hands on his legs, bending at the waist, trying to get Badger to come to him. He finally grabbed Badger's rope and started rubbing his head like nothing happened. "It's okay, boy".

And they take off running back down the road.

I was still hanging onto Mama's chest while she retrieved what was left of the smashed eggs. She cleaned six eggs and handed them to Miss Evans, who shook her hatted head from side to side and sucked her teeth.

"That dog—uh, uh, uh. Cora, I'm gon hafta give you fifteen cents fer de six eggs. Ya broke de others, so I can't pay ya fer a dozen. Brang me a dozen next week an y'all will git yo thirty cents."

Miss Evans turned and headed back down the road.

Mama put the coins in her dress pocket, rubbed dirt into my dog bite, and we walked back down that dusty, dirt road toward home. Miss Evans was the kind of White folk Mama knew, understood, and could get along with.

I just kept thinking about dogs, and how I would hate them forever.

Chapter Six

Working

Before we even moved to 28th Street, Daddy was out there making a garden. He was doing what he did in Mississippi, planting, raking, watering, hoeing. Making crop.

At first, he did all the work by himself. He didn't feel he needed help to work a two-acre garden; he and Mama had made crops on a 240-acre farm!

In our little garden, he wanted Junior, Mae, Leeah, and Ruth to keep doing things like hoeing, planting, and removing grass from plants. He wanted them to remember how to make a garden and to be able "to grow your own food."

When school was out, Daddy would wake up the whole house yelling and turning on lights at 6:30 in the morning: "Mae, Leeah—Y'all git up. I wont dat grass hoed from 'round them greens—git up 'fore it git too hot. Git up."

There was always grumbling, mumbling, turning and twisting, and babies crying.

"I'm tired."

"I don't care 'bout no greens."

I was in the same room with Ruth and in the same bed with Jean. They eased themselves out of bed and prepared to head to the garden. Even Junior answered the call. I was too little to do garden work, so I slept a little longer.

Before long though, all kinds of stuff was growing. Pole beans, squash, watermelon, potatoes, cabbage, greens, onions, and tomatoes were growing in the side garden. Corn was growing in the back.

Sometimes, Miss Fannie would be sitting in her yard. If Daddy or Mama were in the garden, she would make polite conversation.

"Evening. Nice weather we having, ain't it? You got some good-looking greens over there."

Daddy would be mad, but Mama would say, "We's got pleny greens. You welcome anytime ta pick some fer yoself."

Sometimes Miss Fannie would pick a few greens. But mostly, she walked across the road and handed us kids bags of rolls and leftover chicken from her job as a cook at the White country club.

Daddy said she was a "nosy, jealous bitch."

Her food bags did come with a lot of questions: "Did your Daddy git a job yet? He must be getting money from somewhere— Is that a new tree? Looks lak a weeping willa tree."

We didn't know anything. We just said, "Thank you for the food, Miss Fannie."

I was just hoping she put a couple of those little bottles of Coke in one of those bags.

* * *

"Where Daddy goin, Mama?" Mae asked. It was dark outside, and the truck was starting up.

"Your Daddy got a job," Mama said.

"A job? Where? What's he doing?"

"He werking fer the rayroad. At the resterrant."

"Daddy can cook?"

"I don't know wat he doin."

We found out later that he was washing dishes on the overnight shift at L&N train depot restaurant. He said he didn't like the place or the job, but working nights gave him a chance to work in the garden and to look for a better job.

After Daddy got a job working at L&N café, he went against his own vows and got Mama a job there, too.

"Mama, you got a job?" Mae asked.

"Yeah," Mama said, smiling nervously, not covering her mouth like she did when company was around.

"Willie T got me a job."

Mae continued her wide-eyed surprise. "What you goin be doing?"

"He say I gon be cooking."

"You know how to cook resterrant food?"

"I thank so. It jes hamburgers an stuff."

"What you goin wear? How you goin do your hair? So who gon be here wit us? What we suppose to eat? Who gon feed the baby?"

Mama didn't know the answer to none of these questions. She never went nowhere except to Big Mama's house. She just stayed home frying potatoes, soaking and cooking brown beans, washing clothes, and feeding the baby. She could do farming stuff like planting seeds, hoeing grass, picking greens, and she could do all that stuff while watching babies playing and sleeping on a pallet under a shade tree.

She was good at all that stuff. But Mama never worked with White folks. She talked with Miss Evans in Mississippi, but now, she only talked once in a while to Peggy Hines. She'd never even been in a restaurant.

Mama kept asking Daddy questions, "Is dere White peeples cooking too? Wat's dey names? Kin I wear dis blue dress? I ain't got no shoes. I gotta see if Mama can loan me some werk shoes."

Daddy started yelling, "Wat you talkin 'bout, Cora Mae? Dem peckerwoods ain't nobody but po White foks jes lak you. Dey ain't paying no damn 'tention ta you. Old Jimmy and Bobby just trying to make a living jes lak you is. I been dealing wit po peckerwoods all my life. Dey ain't no better den you."

Daddy could talk, cause he worked for White folks and with White folks in Mississippi and in Milwaukee.

"I werk wit anybody, no matter wat dey color is. Some White folks is decent peeples."

We knew the story about the White doctor in Mississippi who stayed up all night to watch over Frank when he was a baby and had double pneumonia. But he also knew White people who he believed had cheated him out of profits when he was a sharecropper. He also felt he was cheated when selling the 240-acre farm in Mississippi.

For Mama, working at L&N restaurant was the first time she ever spent some time around other people besides us kids and Big Mama. Once she started working, she talked about the other workers like they were her new best friends.

She started standing in the front yard talking to Miss Fannie,

"Yea, I'm so tired. I gon try to git some sleep b'for I have ta git up fer werk. I werk wit Billy Ray. We hav so merch fun laffing. And cook, dat boy sho kin fry up dem burgas! All of dem is so funny."

Mama's introduction to the outside world didn't last long. She had to quit when baby number nine was born.

A few months later, Daddy got a better job. He started working nights at Wagner Electric. He said they were making things for cars and airplanes.

Daddy's job was to grind up iron. I know that because we had to shake his overalls upside down extra hard to get out the real tiny pieces of iron that was always in his pockets. He said he"didn't like breathing in all that stuff." So he got a job during the daytime working big machines. Mama was real happy that he got "a good, stirdy job in a factory." That was one of the reasons we left Mississippi.

Chapter Seven

Welcome All!

If people didn't live on 28th Street, it was hard for them to say, "I wuz jes in the neighborhood an thought I would drop by." They had to walk or drive about two or three miles in order to get to our house. That didn't matter, people kept coming by and kept saying, "I wuz in the neighborhood, so I thought I would drop by."

I don't know where they were coming from, but Mama would say, "Come on an set on da porch in de cool. It ain't no trouble a-tall. Jean, go brang a glass of wata."

All kinds of folks were coming by our house. Most of them were trying to sell us stuff. Daddy didn't want nothing to do with "dem crooks."

One week, a sweaty-faced Colored man named Ray, wearing an old, bent up fedora and displaying obsequious manners, came walking by offering us Negro records of gospel singers like Mahalia Jackson. The records had faded pictures on the covers, like they had been rained on. When asked about the "used" covers, Ray tried to add humor by citing the adage, "Don't juge dese records by de covers." The next week, Ray came by selling what he said was coons and possums. They were always skinned and wrapped up in old *Register News* newspapers.

Overweight White men in short-sleeved shirts dropped by in cars offering vacuum cleaners, life insurance policies, and encyclopedias. Mama would welcome them all. They would spread their wares on the front porch. Daddy was a reluctant participant most of the time, but certain offerings caught his attention. He allowed us kids to gather around, but we were not allowed to speak.

Anything having to do with cooking and cleaning was for Mama to decide. "Oh, dis heah a good-looking coon. Kin you brang another possum next week—Willie T, we shor can keep de dirt out wit dis vacum cleana."

Anything having to do with making money and book learning was for Daddy to decide: "You say if we git dis insurance now fer de baby, she kin git mo money back wen she eighteen yeahs ole? Y'all kids kin learn eveythan from des heah encyclopedia books."

It was usually a good day for the salesmen. Coming three miles to 28th Street and unloading most of their wares and getting a cold glass of water was usually well worth the trip.

Then, there was tall, White, round-shouldered Mr. Miller who showed up on our doorsteps in a beige summer suit with a manila folder under his arm, ready to sign us up for "commodities."

Mama asked him: "Why you come ta give us free food? We never ast fer nothin."

He said, "Well, our records show that you have a big family. Let me see."

He looks at papers in the folder and runs a finger over a page.

"Yes, there's eleven of y'all. Is that right?"

From the side of the garage, Ruth, Jean, and I were watching and listening as Mr. Miller looked through his folder and concluded: "Yes, you are entitled to get free food every month."

We kids covered our mouths to temper our excitement. "We gon get free potato chips, soda pops, and maybe, Tootsie Rolls?"

The free food turned out to be canned vegetables, canned beef stew, canned mushy baloney-like stuff, and two long boxes of waxy cheese. Our commodities, except the beef stew, ended up in the tool shed.

Daddy said, "I don't wont no part of this commolicy stuff. We don't need it."

But the food boxes kept coming.

Chapter Eight

Gospel Singing

Once we had that new chest with a radio and a record player in it, Daddy allowed us to listen every Sunday to one of our newly bought gospel music records. And, according to another one of his rules, Mae was the only one who could touch the five records and the record player.

Daddy was at work during the day, and Mama was not inclined to enforce the record-listening rule. She probably didn't know such a rule existed. So, we had already listened to all these records many times during the week.

Yet on Sunday, Leeah, Ruth, and Jean would yell out to Mae from the dining room, "Put on the Blind Boys.—No, we heard them last Sunday.—I wana hear Mahalia Jackson sing 'Precious Lord.' Mae always ended up playing what she wanted, which most of the time was "How I Got Over" by Clara Ward.

We didn't much care what records we listened to. We liked all the songs. We would sing when we were setting the table, when we were eating, and when we were washing the dishes. Sometimes Mama would sing some of the words, too.

I really don't know why we had a piano though. Maybe Daddy was trying to get what he thought rich folks had in their houses. He just said, "Evey house gotta have a piana."

Nobody could play it. It was just another piece of furniture. But it turned out to be the centerpiece of the living room. And it was all because of what was sitting on top of it.

On top on the piano were two white dolls that Jean and I got for Christmas the year before. We thought they were beautiful. Everybody who saw them thought they were beautiful. The perfect place for them then was on top of the piano.

They both had creamy, cherub-white faces, a fixed, red-lipped smile, and brown eyes that opened and closed. Mine was a brunette. She had her hair in pigtails, tied with red and white ribbons to match her dress. The blonde one belonged to Jean. Her hair was also in pigtails, tied with green and white ribbons to match her dress.

Everybody who came to our house would notice those dolls,

"Where did you git dem beautiful dolls?"

"I never seen such pretty dolls befor. Jes beutiful."

With all that celebrity, Daddy said we couldn't play with them.

* * *

The piano rule was "Stay out of the front room unless you are playing the piano."

Each of us were always trying to bang out a tune. So, we were always in the front room.

Jean was the best at banging out tunes. I could finger, "Jesus Loves Me Yes' I Know," but Jean was using both hands to play the whole song. After a while, she could play, "Jesus Keep Me Near the Cross," and "Do You Know Him," and "What A Friend We Have in Jesus." Jean was always on the piano, and the rest of us were always standing around the piano, singing.

At first, we were just singing because it was something to do during those hot summer days. Big Mama heard us sing a few times.

"Y'all too good ta be jes sanging at home. Y'all ought ta be sanging in church."

Miss Fannie heard us and said the same thing, even though she never went to church.

Daddy heard us singing all the time, but he never said anything.

* * *

We were a religious family. And we were a churchgoing family. I don't remember going to church in Mississippi, but I remember saying the Lord's Prayer at home before we went to bed. And we used to bless our food before eating. When we moved to Mt. Vernon and to that little yellow house on 27th Street all that stopped. When we moved into our house on 28th Street, Daddy started taking us to church.

There were so many Black churches in Mt. Vernon to choose from. Most of the churches were near Washington School. Shiloh Baptist was closest to town, near the railroad tracks. That was Big Mama's church. Lively Stone Methodist, Corinthian Baptist, and Pavey Chapel CME were around the corner from Washington School. Farther south of town was Pilgrim Rest Baptist. There were three other "churches" on different street corners opened by bootleg preachers whose names and venues kept changing. There was a Pentecostal church in town that Aunt Helen went to.

We went with Big Mama a few times to Shiloh Baptist church, but Daddy said, "We is Methodist. I want to go to the same 'nomination lik in Mississippi. Our church wuz Sweet Home, CME church. Dat stand fer Colored Methodist Episcopal Church. Dey changed the name from Colored to Christian. So we goin ta Pavey Chapel CME church."

Sundays then were sacred, and Daddy would remind us and himself to "Remember the Sabbath day, to keep it holy." He embraced this scripture fully in terms of his behavior. There was no arguing on Sunday, no cursing, no whoopings, and no working. It was the day when he sat out in the front yard under the weeping willow tree after supper and read the Bible. It was the day to visit and be with family. In the beginning, it was also the day when we could go to the park.

There were some things I liked about church, and there were some things I didn't like. I liked Communion Sundays when the preacher would invite everyone to come kneel at the alter and take 'bread' (cracker) and 'wine' (grape juice). Lots more kids came to church on Communion Sunday. The 'ladies in white' were on duty to slap the hand of boys who reached for two or three glasses of 'wine.' I liked the 'wine' too, but I never reached for two glasses.

I didn't like Sunday school. There were about nine of us kids sitting in the pews listening to our Sunday school teacher, Mrs. Gladys.

"Baby Jesus wuz born in a barn with goats and sheep, and now, Margaret, you read".

That was when I hated Sunday school the most. When Mrs.

Gladys called my name, some of the other kids rolled their eyes and clicked their teeth and blew out a breath real loud. I couldn't help it, cause I got called on to read! I couldn't help it if I was the only one who could read without stopping and stumbling over almost every word!

I liked singing in the kids' choir, but I didn't like rehearsing with kids who wouldn't follow the rules. The boys never stood properly. Mrs. Gladys kept trying: "Jimmy, you and John have to watch my hands. When I raise my hands like this," she raised both hands, slowly, palms up, "you have to stand up with everybody else. Okay. Let's try it again. Everybody watching?"

Everybody was not watching. The boys were not watching.

"Sing loud—open your mouths," Miss Gladys said.

"Now, Margaret is going to be the song leader and everybody else, remember to join in. Okay?" Eyes rolled, teeth clicked, followed by heavy breathing.

The whole choir hated me, except Jean.

The best thing about having so many churches was that something was always going on at one or two of them every Sunday afternoon. There were dinner fundraisers or local gospel singing programs or famous invited guest singers from St. Louis. There was always a church event to go to when we found ourselves all dressed up and needed some place to go besides the park. If it was a church that we wanted to go to, Daddy was always willing to take us.

The first time we sang in church was when our regular church pianist, Mrs. Hart, was sick. The choir seemed lost without her to keep them on key. Daddy was a Deacon. His seat was up front in the first row, and he and the other three men up there were always called on to pray.

When the choir started singing with no music, Daddy stood up and beckoned Jean to come up and play the piano. I was sitting with Jean and other girls she was hoping to become friends with. She gave me "the elbow," which meant she did not want to be called on at this time. She was sitting with her "friends."

Playing the piano was easy for Jean now, because she had been playing church songs at home. And she loved being the center of attention, but not now. There were lots of smiles and affirmations from the congregation as Jean made her way to the piano. She sat down and began to play, "Jesus Keep Me Near the Cross." "Amens" were heard throughout the congregation as the choir sang with enthusiasm. When the choir finished, Daddy stood up again, and this time he announced to the church, "Now my daughters is gon' come up and sang."

What! I was surprised and a little scared. I was looking around at my sisters whose faces held quizzical expressions like, Why is he doing this? None of us moved. Daddy issued a more specific direction.

"Mae, y'all come on up heah an sang."

One by one, Mae first, me last, we walked up and stood in front of the church congregation, three in back, me in front, Jean at the piano. We had not practiced for a performance in church.

Encouraging applause came from the congregation. They didn't know what to expect. We didn't either.

Jean banged out the introduction to "Do You Know Him." Mae, with her smile and head tilt, swayed easily to the beat. Leeah stood confidently tall, swinging her right arm. Ruth stood stiffly, looking straight ahead. I stood in front, not knowing what to do.

With the downbeat from Jean, we sang the way we did everyday at home—loud, spirited, and with an acceptable degree of harmony.

There was loud clapping and "Amens" heard throughout the congregation. If Daddy was pleased, he never let it be known. He was responsible for introducing the Edwards Sisters to the church community and beyond. I wondered why then he wanted to rein us in after more opportunities to sing came knocking.

Chapter Nine

Everybody Likes Jean

Jean and I were best friends. We became best friends when she was in first grade and I was too young to start school. Every day, when she came home, she would run in the house with a book ready to "read" me a story. It was always a story about "the adventures of the big fat lady."

We sat together on the floor in the dining room. Jean opened the book to a random page, closed her eyes, leaned forward, and in a hushed, soft voice began the story.

"Once upon a time there was a big fat lady being chased by a bear—"

I was hanging onto every word as she weaved the story of the fat lady being chased over hills, into caves, and finally escaping in a boat. To my relief, the fat lady always lived on for tomorrow's adventure.

I liked Jean. Everybody liked Jean. Even as a little kid people said, "That child has such beautiful ways."

Jean and I were best friends, but we were very different. I

thought she acted in funny ways; she thought I said funny things. She said nice things about people for no reason; I said nice things about people when they did nice things. She could listen and talk about nothing for hours. I could listen and talk for a while if the topic made sense to me. Jean was "noisy." I was quiet. Jean enjoyed being the center of attention; I preferred being behind the scene. Jean was tall like a "string bean;" I was small and "compact." Jean was more like Mama; I was more like Daddy.

Sometimes Jean would show Mama and Daddy how she could write her ABCs.

"See I got 'good' on my writing."

Daddy would say, "Dat's good."

Soon Mama and Daddy were telling visitors, "Jean sho have good han ritin—let Ms Bertha see you rite."

The "ohs" and "ahs" would follow.

The way Daddy promoted Jean's writing was the second time I ever heard him say something good about anything we did. The first time was when he said to me, "That's right," when I named the carpenter tools correctly.

He rarely said good things about anything we did. I could tell he liked Jean. She made him smile.

One time, I asked Mama, "What was I like when I was a baby?"

"You wuz jes lak you is now, always jes lookin at peeples an not smiling or saying nothin—lak you tryin to figa dem out. You da same now."

* * *

I don't know who invented this game about Mrs. Fatty Tarnes. It was not me; it had to be Jean. But I don't know how it started or why. All I know is that we had a lot of free time, and it was too hot to play outside in the backyard. So, we would hang around in the house with Mama, the babies, and her company.

Ms. Tarnes (Fatty) was our favorite company. She was always trudging over to our house and sitting around talking to Mama. She was too fat to fit in a normal chair, and her thighs would hang over the sides. She put as much of her behind as possible on the chair and spread her knees wide to keep the chair from crashing down or falling over.

She and Mama would sit in the front room talking, "Sho' is hot, ain't it?"

"Shor is. How yo son?" Mama was talking about her boy, Alfie.

"Ah, you know dat boy, he fine as can be."

Smiling all the way, Jean and I would ease onto the floor on each side of Ms. Fatty's chair waiting as the conversation continued.

"—and Chicago, he loves dat city, he want us to come up there, but Cora Mae, we ain't so young anymore."

When we hear, "Better git back on up the hill and make some supper," Jean and I sat up straight, ready. Ms. Fatty spread her legs even wider, leaned forward and squeezed her fat body between her legs as she pushed herself slowly up and up and up.

We dove in for the kill that was, we put our noses to the freshly vacated seat, took a deep breath, and screwed up our faces into the appropriate expression, depending on what smell emanated from the seat.

For me, the smell usually caused immediate eye squinting, nose fanning, and a chawawa face. By the time Ms. Fatty was on her feet and turned around to compliment Mama and us on having such "nice, respectful girls," we were indeed smiling shyly but knowingly.

Chapter Ten

Washington School: Winners & Losers

Jean always talked about her first-grade teacher, Miss Low and all the fun things she did in class. She also said Miss Low was pretty. But when I got to first grade, I don't remember all those fun things Jean talked about, and Miss Low was not pretty. She was just light skinned, tall with skinny legs and had short, pressed hair.

Maybe one reason first grade was not fun for me was because of the Coloring Contest.

One day Miss Low told us, "Class, each of you will get a picture to color. The one who colors the picture the best will win a prize."

I was so excited. I wanted to win the prize. So, I concentrated real hard. I colored this way and that way, up and down, and I was satisfied that I had done a good job. We all handed in our work. There was a White woman in class who was looking at each picture. Her job was to select the winner.

Before naming the winner, Miss Low said, "Class, I hope you

all did the three things you needed to do in order to win."

What three things? I didn't hear anything about three things.

Ms. Low was asking questions, "Did you color in the lines? Did you color in the same direction? Did you color without pressing too hard on the crayon? Raise your hands if you did these three things."

I didn't raise my hand, and I didn't win either. I didn't understand why she was telling us now how to win. I could have been a winner if she had told me the three things I needed to do—before I started coloring.

I didn't like first grade after that.

Maybe I didn't like first grade also because of the cold weather. The memory of the bone-chilling wind, rain, snow, and sometimes ice on that long walk to Washington School was lasting.

But Daddy had a rule about school, and he had a story to go with it: "Y'all is lucky. You kin go ta skool eveyday. Dat's somethin I wuz never able ta do. I don't wont ta ever hear nothing 'bout de cold. I had ta cut wood, git dem cows and hogs fed, an cut pine fer lighting de house. I never got outta second grade."

Before Daddy got the day job at Wagner, he would drive my sisters and Junior to school, especially in the winter. When he moved to working days at Wagner, I started first grade. Walking to school was our only option, except for taking a cab.

In the early years on school days, our morning routine in the winter was always the same: Stay in bed and wait for Daddy to yell into our room, "Y'all get up."

That meant that a fire had been made in the potbelly stove. The time would be about seven o'clock. With a lot of shivering, we would run to the dining room and find a place around the red glow of the stove and warm our behinds. Without moving from the stove, we got dressed, ate our biscuit and gravy, and prepared to walk the three miles to Washington School.

I put on long pants under my dress. I put on my blue wool coat over a sweater. I put a wool scarf on my head and tied it under my chin. I put on my rubber galoshes over my shoes. Mama tied a second woolen scarf around my nose and mouth. And finally, I pulled on my blue gloves. I was now ready to face the elements.

From November to February, I held my head down to keep the wind from a frontal attack on my face. I didn't see the petrified trees dotting our shortcut through the park, and I didn't sneak a peek at the icy lake. I followed my sisters, sometimes walking on the grass, sometimes on the sidewalk, anywhere to avoid slipping and sliding and lagging behind. I arrived at school paralyzed from head to toe.

When I got to class, my routine was always the same. Go to the bathroom and, sometimes with the teachers help, remove my gloves, my scarves, and my shoes. The teacher filled the sink with cold water. I put my frozen hands in the water and waited as the pain of thawing began. My hands and feet were throbbing and aching. My nose was running, and my eyes were tearing. I shifted my body weight from one foot to the other trying to relieve the body aches. After about twenty minutes, I was thawed enough to dry my hands, take off my long pants, put on my shoes, and wipe my face. I exited the bathroom, hung up my pants and coat, arranged my boots and walked to my seat. I was now ready to learn.

One cold, windy, and icy day, Mama decided to order a cab to take me to school. I got in the car with some White guy who didn't seem to know the way to Washington School. He kept driving down streets I had not been on before, and he kept stopping to pick up other people I didn't know. I was told to "move ova an make room fer some mo folks."

There were too many people in the back seat. Some large-hipped White woman who was crushing me and breathing hard started making conversation,

"Ya like school?— Can't walk today—ya got enough room? —More snow tomorrow."

The driver finally found Washington School. He came around to open the door, and I fell out into the snow. I wasn't frozen, but I was late. I hated being late to school.

* * *

Second grade was worse than first grade. It all had to do with my friend Janet and our teacher, Miss Chavis. Janet's mother had died. Her father liked Miss Chavis.

During recess, Janet was jumping rope and talking at the same time, "Miss Chavis was at our house last night, and she's gon marry my daddy".

"No, she ain't," Essie said. "You just saying that cause she pretty."

I was at one end turning the jump rope, and Essie was at the other end. Janet missed and her feet got tangled in the rope. The rule said when that happened, "you're out." It was my turn to jump, and Janet's turn to take the rope. I handed the rope to her. She did not take it.

"I'm not turning. It's still my turn to jump."

"No, it's not. You missed," I said.

"I missed 'cause y'all was talking too much," she claimed.

"Well, I'm not turning no more." I dropped the rope.

"I'm gon tell the teacher," Janet said, and ran into the building.

She came out, "Miss Chavis say you have to come in."

I went into the classroom with confidence ready to tell my side of what happened. Miss Chavis was standing in front of her desk with her long black hair framing her pretty face. *Why is she looking so mad?* Before I could reach her she pointed her finger with red polish on it at my face,

"When you are outside, you are expected to play fair. It seems that you can't play fair, Margaret."

She walked around her desk, opened a drawer and took out a tan-colored wooden ruler. She walked back to me.

"Give me your hand", she said.

I was confused. I kept my hands down.

She grabbed my right hand and turned my palm down to expose my knuckles. I watched her purse her lips as she smacked my knuckles five times with the ruler.

I cringed. My breathing shortened. I winced. A teacher had never hit me before. I'd never even had a whooping.

She released my hand with, "Go sit at your desk and think about what you did."

I reached my desk still confused and rubbing my knuckles. I put my head on my folded arms and, as I was told to do, I thought about what I did. Each thought I came up with was the same: Janet missed, she was supposed to turn the rope, and it was not fair that Miss Chavis hit me with a ruler.

Miss Chavis married Janet's father.

* * *

In third grade, my problem was, "What do I do at lunchtime?" I used to go home with my friend Judy and eat lunch. But after eating three or four lunches of baloney sandwiches and bowls of spaghetti with white bread at her house, her mother told me I couldn't come anymore.

I didn't have money to eat in the cafeteria, so I took my PayDay from my bag and ate it. PayDays were my favorite.

"Margaret, you want to go in town with me and Pat?" Essie asked me. To go would break one of Daddy's rules. I knew I wasn't supposed to leave school unless it was time to walk home.

"Okay, yeah. I'll go."

We left Washington's playground, crossed the railroad tracks, turned right, and went down Grand Street to Woolworth's Five & Dime store. We walked in past White people sitting at the lunch counter. We were not allowed to sit and eat there, because we were Colored.

But Colored folks could come in and spend money on other stuff. So Essie and Pat walked down different aisles, picking up things like necklaces, little dolls on key chains, and balls in a basket. They were looking at earrings attached to little white cards. Essie put a card in her pocket, then Pat. Both made quick steps down the aisle toward the door.

I was perplexed. Should I follow them? I know better, but I grabbed a card, too. Then, I remembered, I have no pockets. I covered the card in my fist. The earring stem was piercing my palm. I was crying inside; I wanted to put the earrings back. I was breaking two rules in one day, Daddy's rule and God's rule: Thou shall not steal. What if I got caught, got thrown in jail, and got a whooping on top of that! I wished I had followed Daddy's rule.

Back at school, beads of sweat on my forehead and breathless, I headed for the bathroom. I opened my fist and saw the bloodstains on the card. I dropped my bounty into the garbage can, covered it with paper towels, and washed my hands real hard. I came out, took my seat and scanned the faces of Pat and Essie. Nothing. Nobody would know about my sins, except God. I would talk to Him about it at church on Sunday.

* * *

"Now class, settle down. Find your seats."

It was my first day in fourth grade at Washington School and my teacher, Mr. Rollins, was speaking to us. I have been looking forward to being in his class. Jean said he's so nice and funny.

I was seated next to my two best friends, Judy and Rosielee. I was wearing a blue church dress with little yellow daisies on it and a white sash tied around my waist with a bow in the back. I bought it in town from Gladstone Department store.

My yellow number two pencil was in the slot at the top of my brown wooden desk, my hands were interlaced on my lap, and my eyes were on the teacher. Mr. Rollins was standing in front of his scarred wooden brown desk with his head tilted slightly to the side. His head was round, his brown hair was cropped real short, and he looked like he was smiling, even when he wasn't. He was wearing his first-day-of-school uniform, a light blue short-sleeved shirt with a collar and one pocket, dark blue pants, and a black belt. I love uniforms.

"Boys." Mr. Rollins gazed over the class looking for attention from the boys that he was not getting. He moved quickly behind his desk, picked up a tan-colored ruler, and slammed it down hard on his desk. That's probably why his desk was so scratched up. There was a stunned freeze in the room. I bet that was the same ruler he used to whack the boys' knuckles, too.

I screwed up my face, looked over my left shoulder, and saw John and Erick pull wayward legs under their desks. I was full up with confidence as I put on my smile of satisfaction. I approved of Mr. Rollin's being strict with the boys.

He continued, "You are now in the upper school. You are expected to follow my rules. Number one: No talking unless you—"

I was used to rules. Mr. Rollins was a lot like my Daddy. When somebody broke one of Daddy's rules, that's when he grabbed the switch from behind the stove and that person got a whooping. It was usually Ruth. She kept talking back, and she never did what she was told to do. And she didn't seem to care. She got welts all over her legs and arms, but the next day she did something again. Leeah also got whoopings a lot for "talking so damn much." She did not listen and talked back a lot.

"—understand the rules."

I paid attention.

Mr. Rollins was glancing at a clipboard in one hand and holding a yellow number two pencil in the other.

"We are going to go over some spelling words first."

I was good at spelling. He could ask me anything.

"Harry, how do you spell 'stomach'?"

"S—t—u—" Mr. Rollins scanned faces as he walked slowly down the first row of desks.

"Rosielee, how do you spell 'stomach'?"

"S—t—o—m—o—"

Hands were waving in the air; bodies were raised out of seats, and hands were covering mouths. There was no talking: Rule Number Three.

I was among the hand wavers. Mr. Rollins continued to pace, eyeing the room and calling on Jerri.

"Stumack."

Some of the girls had hands together under their chins in silent prayer, hoping Mr. Rollins would call on them. I decided to save my prayer for something bigger than "stomach."

Mr. Rollins continued to survey the room as if looking for someone in particular. His eyes landed on Judy.

"Judy, how do you spell 'stomach'?"

Judy stood, smoothed down her plain apple green dress, looked around at the rest of us, put on a smile of success, and spoke, pronouncing each letter slowly and precisely.

"S—t—o—m—a—c—h. Stomach."

Her smile remained as she again smoothed the skirt of her apple green dress and slid into her chair. Waving hands and praying hands returned to their resting positions. Mr. Rollins glared at the rest of us, stabbing at the air with his number two yellow pencil from one side of the room to the other. Through narrow, squinty brown eyes, he announced to the class,

"Finally, I have found my dictionary."

"What?" I thought.

Jean said Mr. Rollins was nice, but he was not. I was starring at him. I looked around the class to see how others were taking this announcement. The girls were either pouting with their lower lip pushed out or resting their heads on an elbowed hand. The boys had either a wide-eyed, mouth hanging open look of "What just happened?" or they were fiddling with that number two pencil, trying to get it to stay in the slot on the desk.

I brought my gaze back to Mr. Rollins' round head and toothy grin. I was mad. I knew how to spell "stomach." I was just as smart as Judy—everybody knew that. I was hoping that this year would be different, that maybe there would be no "dictionary" this year.

Judy was the "dictionary" in Ms. Brown's third grade class. What made Judy stand out was the color of her skin. She was "high-yellow." She had the lightest skin in the whole school. I think teachers liked light-skinned kids.

Judy's family lived down the street from Mr. Rollins and across the street from the school. Her big sister Bella had been in Mr. Rollins' class. Judy's family went to the same church as the Rollins family. Plus, Judy was tall for a fourth grader, and she was smart.

I had no chance of being the teacher's "dictionary," if being 'high yellow' was one of the criteria. I was short, and my skin was dark brown, and I didn't stand out in a crowd. I lived on 28th Street in the "country," and I walked three miles every day to school. When I got to school frozen in the wintertime, the kids laughed at me and asked, "Why do you live way out there in the country?" I had nobody in my class to play with after school. This was only my second day in fourth grade, but I was smart, and I had deep thoughts about fairness.

Chapter Eleven

All About Family

Daddy didn't talk a lot. He never shared his feelings about any of us or about anything we did. Maybe he felt he didn't have to, since he had put in place lots of rules, and rules said exactly what you are supposed to do and how everybody was supposed to behave, so a lot of talking was not necessary. My sisters did not like the rules and sometimes argued and fussed and yelled and didn't always follow them.

Daddy worked a lot and we had what our large family needed. He was all about family, especially the ones on his side of the family. No matter how lazy, down and out, or jealous, anybody in his family was, he was there for them.

It took about six months after we left Mississippi for Uncle Lester and Aunt Erma and my six cousins to follow us to Mt. Vernon.

Daddy just said, "Lester shoulda stayed in Mississippi an farmed dat land. I give him everthan fer a real good start."

Mama said, "He come up heah to Mt. Vernon, Willie, because

yo brother is lazy, and he expect you to keep taking care of him."

Mama was talking about the eleven years in Mississippi she and Daddy spent supporting his brother Lester, her sister Erma, and their kids. When Daddy bought the 240-acre farm, it included a large log house, a smaller house, a barn, and a pond.

Daddy partitioned the large log house in half and allowed his brother and family to move into one side. According to Daddy, "We had to live wit dem 'cause Lester wuz gonna starve hisself an his whole family."

When Lester and Erma would not get to the fields to help make crop, Mama and Daddy worked extra hard to make up the difference. When planting season was over, Daddy sold timber and worked at the tire plant. Lester proclaimed himself a preacher and spent his time reading the Bible, talking scripture and making excuses. After Daddy left Mississippi, Lester never made another crop.

Uncle Lester and the family arrived at Big Mama's house with no money, no place to live, and no plans for how they were going to make a living. Big Mama said they could stay in her one-room guesthouse "for a while." They stayed there a year, and would have stayed longer if Daddy had not rescued them once again.

When Uncle Lester and family first came to our house, Ruth and Leeah were covering their mouths laughing and pointing at them. I didn't know who these people were. They were some raggedy-looking people.

So, I asked Mama, "Who is these visitors?"

Mama said, "Dese your cousins from Mississippi. Don't you 'member dem?"

No, I did not remember these people. Everything about these cousins was ashy, like they never heard of Vaseline! Everybody knows you never leave the house without greasing your arms and legs. Maybe they forgot, because their faces, their arms, their legs, and their feet were white with ash. They looked like they had walked to Mt. Vernon from Mississippi.

I did remember Louise, the oldest girl. She was Ruth's friend, and they were both eight years old. Louise was dressed in a greyish sack-like covering that was tied around her waist with a string. The youngest girl, Bea, about two years old, had no plaits, just packed-down nappy hair. She was whining and clinging to Aunt Erma's skirt tail. The three oldest boys, Roy, BB and Gilbert in their short overalls were just standing and staring. Then the three of them started running down the road, punching each other and kicking up a lot of dust.

Sam, who was about five, kept digging fists full of dirt out of the pockets of his overalls and throwing it in our direction. Uncle Lester's pants were being held up with red suspenders that were the same color as his gums. Aunt Erma, with her head tied up with a blue and brown head rag, looked like the slave woman in our encyclopedia. She and Sam had the same darting eyes. Plus, all of them were speaking a foreign language.

Louise said to Ruth, "Wat tat?"

Ruth said to Louise, "What?"

Sam said to Jean, "Y'all libe heah?"

Jean said, "What?"

"Wat cho nam?"

"Wat chu laffin et?"

I was not laughing at them. I just wondered if we looked like that and talked like them when we got out of our truck at Big Mama's house six months ago.

Uncle Lester kept talking, gesticulating and staring at our new house.

"I'se looking for a job so I kin git my family a place to live. There ain't no jobs out der. I went to de park. I went to the rayroad. Wat else kin I do? The Bible says in First Timothy: 'Anyone who does not provide for his relatives, and their own household, has denied the faith and is worse than a unbeliever.' You see what I'm saying—I kin work. I know my Bible. A man kin only do so merch."

Daddy never called his brother a trifling misfit, but Mama sure did. Daddy knew Lester was never going to leave Big Mama's house unless, like before, he was given a house to live in.

Daddy bought a piece of land down the street next to Mrs. Fannie and started building a house for Uncle Lester and his family. Before he set off each night to work at L&N café, and later to Wagner, Daddy worked on the house and told Uncle Lester what work he should do to help complete the job.

One time when I was there with Daddy, he said to his brother, "Lester, you wuz supose to bring Roy and BB to help put up dis drywall in dis bedroom."

Uncle Lester looked around smiling, his red gums showing, and his hands flared in helpless disbelief, "I kin do de werk—no problem wit dat. You know how young peeples is dese days—dey don't wont to do certain thangs. What I'se supos to do! Wat did the Bible say in Thessalonians 3:10. It says, 'If a man will not work, he shall not eat.' Ya see, I nos the Bible. Tell me what you want me to do, and I'll do it. Ain't that wat it says? Margaret, ain't that wat it says?"

I shrugged.

Daddy grabbed hold of the drywall. "Lester, hand me the

hammer and some nails."

Looked like Daddy didn't need me to hand him things, so I left and went home.

Months later, when the family moved in, Uncle Lester was still quoting scriptures while bed sheets hung as dividers between the three bedrooms.

* * *

When our cousins moved in down the street, I thought, "Now we have someone else to play with."

Ruth and Louise were the same age, and they were always together. The only cousin around my age was Sam, and he was a boy. He didn't want to dress up and play house.

He came to our house anyway. We could hear him coming, doing boy things and making boy noises. He was hitting the side of the garage with little rocks and splashing in the dirty ditch water on the side of the road. He showed up grinning with his eyes darting back and forth like a bullfrog. And for no reason at all, he walked up to me and hit me in my stomach. Plus, he thought it was funny seeing me fold over in pain. He hit me almost every day!

I didn't know what to do. Jean told me I should squat down when he came, so he couldn't hit my stomach. So, the next day we were outside making mud pies, talking to and feeding them to our corncob dolls with corn silk hair, when I looked up and saw Sam headed in our direction. I stayed in my squat position with my eyes on my doll.

I hear him say, "Wats dese silly thangs?"

He then plants both bare feet into our freshly made mud

pies. "What you do that for? Stop it."

I stood up.

He rushed in and gave me a solid punch to the stomach.

"Ouch, ohhhh. I'm gon tell Aunt Erma."

I crouched over in pain as he ran, laughing, up the road toward his house.

I had to do something.

"I'm gonna tell Aunt Erma."

Jean said. "She's just like Sam. She ain't gon do nothing."

The only person who could do something was Ruth. I didn't want to tell her though, since she was always getting in trouble herself. I just wanted to play outside in the backyard and not have to be on the lookout for Sam. So, I told Ruth that he was always punching me in the stomach.

She just said, "He better stop doin dat."

The next day, Jean, Ruth, and I waited for Sam to show up. When he reached the backyard, Ruth stepped up and grabbed him from behind by his overall straps and pinned his arms to his back.

"Wat chu doin? Let me go." Sam was kicking and trying to wrestle out of Ruth's arms.

She was holding on and said to me, "Margaret, go to it."

And I did. I hit him in the stomach two times, but not too hard 'cause tears were running down his face and snot was running out of his nose. Ruth held him up real close to her face then and asked him, "Do you wont me ta step on you and mash you up like a dirty June bug?"

Sam's toes were barely touching the ground, his arms were dangling by his side like a ragdoll, and his eyes were dancing wildly, here and there.

"Naw, naw," he managed to say between sniffles.

"Den you better not put yo hands on her agin." She pointed at me. She dropped him.

He hit the ground like a sack of potatoes, flailing this way and that in the dust and dirt trying to get to his feet. He ran off, looking back to see if Ruth was coming after him.

Ruth smacked her hands together. I smiled; glad she didn't rough him up too much.

He never hit me again. The back yard was safe again—for now.

* * *

One summer, Mrs. Fanny's grandson, B.J. came from Chicago to visit her. He was six years old. He stayed at our house to play when Mrs. Fanny went to work at the White country club.

He became our little brother, but he did not always want to play in the mud or walk in the ditch water.

One time he asked me if I wanted to play a game.

I said, "Okay."

He said, "It's 'bout a movie."

I said, "You talkin bout a movie show? I never saw no movie show."

He said, "All ya do is lay on da floor and pull yo dress up."

Oh, I thought, *Is he talking 'bout 'playing nasty'? Mama always told my sisters 'Don't y'all be 'playing nasty' now.'*

I never played nasty before, so I said, "Okay."

We went to the tool shed and closed the door.

BJ said, "We gon do wat dey do in the movies."

I lay down on the cold concrete floor and pulled up my dress.

It was not Sunday, so I wasn't wearing bloomers. BJ unbuckled his overalls and let them drop to his ankles. He wasn't wearing bvds, either. He lay on top of me with his "between the legs" on top of my "between the legs."

"Now," BJ said, "I kiss yo face like dis."

"And what I'm supose to do in this movie?" I wanted to know.

"You don't do nutin," he said.

After about a minute of kissing spit on each side of my face, I was dripping wet. Spit was running into my ears. I felt like I was drowning. 'Playing nasty' was dangerous.

"I don't like this movie game," I said.

So B.J. got up, pulled up his overalls, and hooked the straps. I got up, still wiping spit from my face, pulled down my dress, and wiped some more spit off with my dress. B.J. opened the door, and we both left the shed. We still had a pile dirt and some water, so we went back to making mud pies.

After that, I didn't want to go to no more movie shows.

* * *

One evening, a cousin of Daddy's showed up at our house saying, "I know you lived in Mt. Vernon, so I thought I would stop by for a visit."

From the looks of him, he must have walked a long way to get to our house, because he was dirty, smelly, and all he had with him was a brown crocus sack with his clothes and stuff in it.

His name was Jacob. He was tall, dark-skinned, and younger-looking than Daddy. He appeared shy and smiled a lot. Daddy was happier "to see family" than I had seen him in a long while. He was grinning and talking. He was puffed up with pride.

"Let me show you the place."

They walked the property, the backyard, up the hill to the pigpen, and down the road past the neighbors' houses. I saw Daddy pointing, talking, and laughing. When they returned home, they started telling stories about Mississippi and about Jacob's parents. Daddy was offering food and more food.

"Come on, boy. Eat. We got plenty."

When it was time to sleep, Daddy said, "I don't have family come heah eveyday. An wen someone from my family come ta visit, I wont dem ta have de best. You gon sleep in our bedroom."

Jacob was trying to refuse, saying, "Oh no, no, I don't want to put you out of your room." He was heading to the corner to pick up his brown bag. "I can sleep—"

Daddy cut him off. "Eny relation of mine gits de best."

Mama was staring at Daddy with bug-eyes, trying to get his attention. Her mind was running through the "moving to another room" scenario. We all, including me, were thinking the same thing. Daddy and Mama with her big stomach, and the baby move to our room; we kids move to pallets on the floor. Seven kids who had to get up for school in the morning, dress, eat, and get out the door. And all this for a cousin with everything he owned in a crocus sack!

Daddy avoided Mama's wide eyes of disbelief and forged right ahead, "Cora Mae an me wont you ta enjoy our hospitality."

Two days later, Jacob was still enjoying our hospitality. He was sleeping late in a clean comfortable bed, eating breakfast, lunch, and dinner and taking strolls up and down the road greeting the neighbors, having snack breaks with Mama and keeping her company while she cooked, fed babies, and kept his sack full of clothes clean and ironed.

Daddy came home tired and dirty from working all day and was greeted by a relaxed, clean-shaven Jacob, ready to hear more family stories before he sat down for another good supper of what he called "down home" food. One thing he never talked about was where he came from and when he was planning to leave.

It took three days for Daddy to realize that something was not right about his cousin Jacob. I don't know exactly what happened, but I was evesdropping that night and heard Daddy and Mama talking.

"He come here walking—he just out of prison over there in Vandalia—No suitcase—He gotta leave."

When we got home from school the next day, Jacob was gone.

* * *

Daddy was always talking about his family up North. He said his mother and father, his oldest brother, David and two of his sisters, Helen and Mattie lived in St. Louis. He said they all lived right over the bridge.

"So we have some more cousins, besides Louise and Sam and dem?" Ruth wanted to know.

"You got a lot of cousins and relations ret there in St. Louis."

"Can we go to their house, can we? Can we?" We were jumping around so excited. We got some more cousins!

So, one summer Sunday, Daddy loaded us in the truck and we headed to St. Louis to meet his family and our cousins.

The best part of the trip for me was the view from the back of the truck.

I love seeing field after field of hay, loaded stalks of corn, and cloudy blue skies that disappeared in the distance. Sitting with my sisters, we waved to truck drivers and they waved back. I saw a tall statue of a church lady with her hand raised toward the sky. We crossed over a big bridge with a river of rushing water underneath. This must be the bridge Daddy was talking about. I looked down and saw a lot of little people living under the bridge. I never saw or heard of people so little. Daddy never said anything about these people. They were walking, driving cars and riding in sailboats on the river! I would really like to visit that city some day and see these little people up close.

Daddy pulled the truck up and stopped in front of a row of red brick buildings with lots of steps leading up to doors at the top. The steps reminded me of the clapboard apartment house we walk by on our way to Washington School. Both places had teenage boys in plaid shirts leaning on railings, talking and eyeing giggling girls sitting on the steps. Both places had little kids running, tussling and screaming at each other in a small front yard. Everybody is Colored.

I don't know who lives in this one apartment we go into. But the ten of us add to the traffic of people moving back and forth between over-stuffed chairs in the living room and the over-flowing food table in the dining room. There are a lot of hugs and wet kisses and offers to "Come on in..." "Git a plate."

We met Uncle David. He looked a lot like Daddy. Mama said later on, "He ain't nothing lak yo daddy. He's lazy. Ever since I knowed him, he been sayin he too old to werk."

"Y'all so big."

"Set down"... "We got plenty."

Me and Jean met Aunt Mattie and was looking around for our cousins. She said, "These yo cousins Dean and Lee ret over there." I saw two ladies. "And Dale is bout yo age, he yo cousin too." Dale was about nine, but he was just sitting by himself. I don't think he wanted to talk or play or anything.

That must be Grandma Edwards sitting at one end of the food table. She was dark with broad shoulders and grey hair. She was just sitting, eating, not talking. The small guy having no trouble getting a lot of laughter out of Dean and Lee had to be Big Papa. I had heard about him.

I guess this house must belong to Aunt Helen and Uncle Jay since they were the only ones busy clearing plates and keeping the food coming. I didn't meet them.

Jean and I finally got some food and sat together with plates on our laps, eating with our fingers because "we is family."

I watched Daddy. His family brought out a different side of him. He was laughing, slapping his leg, eating and telling stories, "We couldn't swim a lick, but we jumped in dat river anyway, we wuz crazy." "And what about dat ole peckerwood at da sawmill?" "Remember Dee Bery? Dat man could pick cotton... three or four bales a hour!"

Mama was smiling and talking to whomever she could get to. I could tell she was just glad to be out of the house and be around grown people that she knows. She was saying things like, "I'm so glad to see everybody. It's ben so long. Dean, las time I saw you, you wuz a lil' ole thang."

I give Jean 'the elbow', which means 'keep a straight face'. There is nothing little about Dean now. Her fat is spreading over the sides of her chair like Ms. Fatty's.

Mama keeps talking,

"How you, Mrs. Edwards? It's so good to see you and Mr. Edwards. Y'all welcome ta come ta Mt. Vernon... any time. We got plenty room."

Junior and Mae know all these relatives. They are in conversation with Lee. Mae is looking around the room and Junior is nodding a lot.

When we can't eat anymore, and the family stories have dried up for now, we raised our hands to wave 'good-bye.' Daddy stopped us, "Y'all can't go nowhere without asting your grandparents about they health. Dat's jes good mannas. Come on an ast dem how dey feeling and tell dem you hope dey feeling good."

When Daddy started talking about 'good mannas,' Junior, Mae and Leeah bolted for the door. Me, Jean and Ruth are the ones left who are old enough to understand what we are supposed to say.

One at a time, the three of us asked, "How you feeling, Grandmother and Big Papa?"

We didn't wait for an answer. Each of us just said the words and headed for the door. I didn't understand Daddy sometimes. He wanted us to check on his parent's feelings, but he never checked on ours! I guess this is what you do when you got relatives around who are old.

We climbed up on the back of the truck holding on to paper plates piled high with potato salad, fried chicken, macaroni, and cheese and apple pie. There was not much talking on the ride home. We were just trying to maintain our balance when Daddy sped around curves and potholes. I was thinking about Daddy and how happy he was with his family; he was enjoying himself so much he lost track of the time. Now he is in a hurry. He wants to get across the Bridge before dark.

* * *

During the year that Uncle Lester and his family were moving into their unfinished house, Daddy bought another piece of land. This small lot was next to the White church on the 29th Street wagon path and a short walk through the cornfield in the back of our house. This new house was for Aunt Helen, Uncle Jay, Grandmother, and Big Papa.

Daddy never said anything to any of us about building another house or that his parents were moving to Mt. Vernon. I don't think Mama knew either. There were a lot of questions that needed answering, like where was the money coming from to do all this building for his family? We all knew that Uncle Lester "didn't have a pot to piss in." And how was Aunt Helen able to build a new house on a cleaning lady's salary? That was probably one of the reasons Mama and Daddy were doing all that yelling every Friday night and Saturday morning. Mama probably wanted answers.

Daddy found the time to work on Aunt Helen's house during the day when he worked nights at Wagner Electric. When the building was underway, Uncle Jay came over for a week or two and slept in the house or in our shed to be around to help out. He couldn't do heavy lifting or be in the sun too long, because according to Mama "He got pilepsi and can fall down when he hav' a fit". Nobody could tell when he was going to have one, so that's why he couldn't get a regular job. That's why he was always home during the day, just sitting around with Mama in the dining room, talking, laughing, and drinking coffee out of a saucer.

To help them move to Mt. Vernon, Daddy made a couple of trips to St. Louis by himself to bring back furniture and beds. When they moved in, we were surprised to see that Dale, Aunt Mattie's twelve-year-old son, had come as well. He stayed to himself and never came to our house. I think he was depressed because his mother gave him to Aunt Helen to raise so she could go to live and work in New York City.

When Aunt Helen moved into her new house, I knew right away that she was a witch. She was the oldest of the ten children in Daddy's family. She didn't have her sisters' big-boned stoutness and their dark skin. She had all the characteristics of a witch. She had a pointed nose, like White people; she always wore a hat and long dresses; she had a slim build and brown skin, and she was seen quite often out walking at night. And, she was mean to kids, and to Uncle Jay who was a tall, thin, kind man.

Aunt Helen knew Uncle Jay had epilepsy when she married him and that he couldn't work. But she was angry with him all the time because he was not working. She was always bossing him around in front of us.

"Jay, get your sorry self up and bring in some firewood.—You still drinking coffee? I guess you can see the grass needs to be mowed."

Uncle Jay would just get up and bring in the wood and continue sipping his coffee. He said nothing about the grass.

When Grandmother was sick, Daddy made Jean and me go with him to see her. Aunt Helen always talked nice to Daddy, because he built her a house for free.

"Hey T, come on in."

The house was the same as always, dark and dank with

windows and white curtains closed. I knew I was going into a witch's lair. Before we even get into the front door, Aunt Helen was giving us instructions: "You kids take yo shoes off, I don't wont mud on my flo—don't set on the couch, use them two chairs."

Uncle Jay ignored her, "Don't worry about the mud, sit down. Y'all wont something to eat?"

He was looking from me to Jean. I cough once, which is our code for "Yes." I could feel the witch's eyes squinting and fixing on Uncle Jay. We lined up behind him and marched into the kitchen.

One thing I must say about Aunt Helen: She may have been a witch, but that witch sure could cook. She made the best homemade biscuits. And with her in the living room with Daddy, and with me and Jean in the kitchen with Uncle Jay, that basket of hot biscuits was free for the taking.

We take two each. I carefully pry each biscuit open and spread butter on each of the four halves. Butter was dripping over my hands almost to my elbows. Then came the grape jelly, my favorite. I spread a thick layer over the buttered halves. Then I gingerly put the halves back together. I held the first biscuit up level with my mouth, closed my eyes, and opened my mouth wide in anticipation.

"Jay!"

I opened my eyes, saw the witch, closed my mouth, held on to my biscuit, but lost my appetite. She was yelling at Uncle Jay.

"Sometimes, I thank you ain't all there! You feeding dem dinner!"

I was looking from Jean, to Uncle Jay, to the witch who was now hovering over the table, grabbing the basket of biscuits to her chest like an angry buzzard protecting its prey. I dropped my biscuit and pushed myself into the back of the chair, gave Jean a "foot kick" code, which meant "get up and run."

Daddy caught us on the way out. We were led into Grandmother's bedroom. I stumbled like a blind cat, cradling the wall for support but managing to remember what we came up here for.

"How you feeling, Grandmother?"

Ruth, Leeah, and Mae didn't have to come to see Grandmother to pose the question. They always had homework to do.

* * *

Before Grandmother got sick, and even after she got sick, Daddy was the only family, besides Aunt Helen, who saw his mother on a regular basis. Uncle Lester was never seen visiting Grandmother Edwards, nor did Uncle David come over to visit.

Big Papa was always around, mostly hollering out pleasantries to everybody in the neighborhood. He still saw himself as 'a gentleman and a ladies' man' in his grey fedora, brown suit jacket and pants from days gone by. But that was not the reputation that followed him from Mississippi to St. Louis to Mt. Vernon.

I don't think Daddy ever got over the hardship and desperation he experienced when growing up dirt-poor in Mississippi. Daddy told us the story:

"I hate to say it, but I didn't hav a good father. He wuzn't no farmer an he sho wuzn't gon pick no cotton. Nobidy knows where he wuz haf de time. He wuz gon fer days. Den he come home an be yelling about 'makin crop'. We kids had to get up fore day brak an go to dem fields to pick cotton an watever. Wen we finished de werk, we could go to skool. Some fathers cut firewood, but my daddy—he wouldn't cut no wood. So, we boys had ta stop skool ta cut de wood an we had ta git da cows an hogs up.

"Sometimes we had no kerosene fer light. So, we had ta go ta de woods an cut pine for light—dat the only light we had for readin. So, if we wuz lucky, we went to skool 'bout two or three days a week.

"Wen I wuz twelve years old, my daddy took me, David, an Lester outta skool fer good an sent us ta werk in the sawmills to make money. Dis went on til I wuz 'bout fourteen yeahs old. I don't know how we made it. We couldn't grow nothin. We had to feed the mules sawdust. After two yeahs, I lef home an went ta Greenville, Mississippi, an got me a job on de railroads. Wen I wuz in Greenville, I wonted ta go back ta skool an go ta collige. I wuz still in second grade. De principal say I missed too merch skool."

In Mt. Vernon, Big Papa spent his time walking. He walked through the cornfield to our house; he walked up the hill to the Tarnes', and he walked across the wagon path to Miss Mary's house. He spent a lot of time at Miss Mary's, a Black woman who built a small house on the corner of Fishers Lane and across from the White church. Mostly though, he sat in his yard or on our front porch listening to Brooklyn Dodgers baseball games.

He and Daddy never talked much. They seemingly didn't have much to talk about. The only thing I remember them doing together was slaughtering hogs in the backyard. Early in the morning, I listened to squealing and pounding, and when I looked out the window, all I saw was a sledgehammer and two halves of a dead hog draining blood into a trough. I wonder which one of them was the teacher in the slaughtering of that hog, Big Papa or Daddy.

Big Papa was not a churchgoer, but Grandmother was. She was one of the "ladies in white." She was tall and "stout." She went with us to Pavey Chapel every Sunday. I never got to know her. She never talked to us. Daddy was a lot like her.

When she got sick, it was Daddy who visited her everyday. It was Daddy who drove her to doctors' appointments. It was Daddy who drove her to clinics in Kentucky and Tennessee and St. Louis, in search of treatments for her high blood pressure and diabetes. Grandmother died when I was ten years old. Big Papa started spending even more time at Miss Mary's.

* * *

Our cousins Dean, Lee, and Uncle David still lived in St. Louis. So Daddy decided one Sunday afternoon to pile us in the truck and go visit them. Big Papa was invited to come along. He sat on his favorite chair on the back of the truck while us kids sat on the floor on pads. We had not visited St. Louis for a while and was surprised when we had to stop halfway across Eads Bridge at a toll booth. I hear Daddy ask the man, "Wat's goin on heah."

The man answers, "Ya have to pay a toll to cross—look at de sign."

Daddy replies,"I been coming to St. Louis for yeahs and never had to pay no toll. How merch is de toll?"

"Ya pay by de head. How many people you got in there? One, two—I count ten, babies are free—that'll be $10.00.

"Ten dollars? I ain't got no $10.00 fer no toll. Dat's too merch money."

"That's what you gotta pay if ya wanna cross—you're holding up the line."

"Well, I can't pay it—I ain't got no $10.00."

"Then ya can't cross. Ya gotta turn around."

"Turn around? Man, you crazy. How I'm gon turn dis truck 'round on dis bridge? Let me go thew and turn—"

"No, can't let ya through. If ya can't pay de toll, ya gotta turn around—Let's go".

We had been listening to this back and forth. Daddy was gonna have to turn this truck around on this bridge!

The man came out of the booth and put up his hand to stop the two-way traffic. We couldn't hear him, but I know Daddy was calling that man every name from 'peckerwood' to 'White bastard' to 'son-of-a-bitch'—even though it was Sunday. The man started using hand signals to help Daddy turn our flatbed truck around. He beckoned Daddy forward with his hand, and moved him back with his hand. Daddy couldn't see how much to back up so he banged into the bridge one time, two times—I stopped counting. Big Papa was holding on to the side of the truck and each time the truck banged into the side of the bridge yelled, "Whoa boy," "Whoa." "Whoa." I covered my mouth to keep from screaming.

White drivers and families sitting in the traffic jam were staring and sneering because they had to wait for "a truck full of poor Colored folks (or niggers) with no money for the toll to turn around on the bridge." Little kids with their eyes wide and their heads sticking out of car windows grinned and stared as their parents pointed and explained. Drivers from both directions began a cacophony of honking their horns. I lowered myself further down to an almost prone position on the bed of the truck in an effort to limit my exposure to the noise and the stares. I was embarrassed, and humiliated. After ten minutes of back and forth and bang after bang, the turn was completed. I could finally raise my head.

We kept our thoughts to ourselves as we made our way home. We didn't visit St. Louis again for a long while.

* * *

Aunt Belle was Mama's sister, but Daddy treated her like family. When he was a farmer in Mississippi, she invited him to Milwaukee "to make money because there are so many jobs up here." He went to Milwaukee, worked in a factory for two months, made a lot of money, but came back home to Mississippi. He said, "I couldn't stay up dere. Too many peoples. Folks wuz out all day an night talkin an playin music. Dem peoples never went to bed. I didn't lak it up dere."

To me, Aunt Belle was a movie star and a glamor girl. Her face was not pretty, but she always had on powder, red rouge and matching red lipstick. Her fingernails were always painted red, and her hair was always "done." She was dark skinned and not real skinny, but she dressed so sophisticated.

She lived in Detroit. Her husband drove her to our house in a shiny new black car. We were not allowed in the front yard, so Jean and I squatted on the side of the house "oohing and aahing" at every move she made. She waited in the car until her husband came around to open her door.

The first part of her emerging from the car was one brown leg with stockings, and a black patent leather pump on her foot. Her stocking seam was perfectly straight.

I could not contain myself. "Ooh, whew. Ooh, ooh look at that—"

The other leg followed. There standing before us was all of

her. Her pressed and curled hair just touching her earlobes, that big smile, and a flared green dress with a black patent leather belt that matched her shoes.

Jean and I kept pushing each other trying to get a better view. We watched her sashay across the walkway between the two brick pillars, up the steps and onto the porch. She hugged Mama, shook hands with Daddy, and introduced her new husband. With her "up North" English, she asked, "Where are the kids, Sista? I want to see them."

Mama answered, "Dey hidin somewhea. I know dey be out in a short whil."

I was thinking, "Why is Mama talking so country and covering her mouth! Why can't she be sophisticated, like Aunt Belle! Why can't she stand up tall and stop wearing those old dresses? Where are her pumps? This is so embarrassing!"

"Margaret, Jean, why are you hiding from me? Come on over here and give me a hug."

She saw us. I was wearing my church blue dress, my brown church shoes, and some bloomers. Her hugs were so tight, and she smelled like peppermint candy.

"I'm so glad to see you. Let me look at you."

I wasn't used to having anybody look at me, so I stood there playing with my fingers and twisting my skirt from side to side, hoping she would move on to Jean. She didn't.

"How old are you, Margaret?"

"Six."

She is laughing now showing her straight white teeth.

"Nooo, nooo! With those legs? You got to be older than that. I tell you, Sista, this child has got the prettiest legs I have ever seen—And just six years old!—Watch out, Sista. Jean— just look at you—You are—"

I stopped listening and just focused on looking at her. She was smiling, laughing, touching her husband's arm, and carrying her body so straight in those pumps.

I wore pumps, too. So, she had nothing on me wearing pumps, except hers were prettier than mine. I wore Mama's old black pumps, since she never went anywhere.

I wore pumps all the time, except today. I never had any trouble wearing my pumps. I wore them playing house in the backyard, I wore them up the hill with Mama to milk the cow, and I wore them to chase down hoppergrasses and snake doctors. I wore them with Jean through the park to the White grocery store on Perkins Street. White people driving by in their cars with the windows rolled down always pointed and laughed at me. I didn't care.

Aunt Belle brought all that city sophistication to our house every time she came. I wanted to be sophisticated like her. I kept practicing how to walk up straight in my pumps.

Chapter Twelve

Park Sundays, The Numbers & Santa

When we first moved to 28th Street, being so close to the city park was a lifesaver. The park had everything we needed. And the best part was, we were allowed to go there every Sunday after church. There were rules though: All the work around the house had to be done on Saturday, and nobody could do anything to get a whooping.

My sisters rose early to wash clothes, hang out clothes, and iron clothes. They cleaned the house, mopped floors, wiped blinds, and helped pick greens and shell peas. Sometimes, Mama liked to add poke salad greens to turnip greens. She looked for the grass in the tall weeds up the hill. I tagged along to see what poke salad looked like and to help her pick it.

And Saturday afternoons was 'whipping out the flies' day. There were a lot of flies around our house, mostly because they loved sitting on our cow Lucy and hanging around the chickens in the yard. But flies also love greens, especially collard greens.

Every time mama cooked collards, all kind of flies, big horseflies and little baby flies would come from everywhere, humming and sticking to our kitchen screen door trying to get into the house. When that door opened, those flies would rush in. Mama was always yelling, "Y'all stop opening dat door. You letting all dem flies in dis house." She had to make sure that lid on the pot of collards was on real tight.

Leeah was in charge of whipping the flies out of the house. Mae, Leeah, Ruth, and Jean each got a rag or a towel and went first to the rooms with doors and swatted at low hanging flies to drive them out of hiding and into the open spaces like the dining room and front room. But flies are smart. They would go up to the ceiling and hide cause they thought my sisters wouldn't look up there. But after whipping out flies every week, my sisters got smart, too. They started standing on a chair to get to those flies.

There was no door between the living room and the dining room. There was no kitchen door either. That was my chance to stand in one of those doorways and swing my rag in a circle like a "windmill" to keep the flies from re-entering de-flied spaces.

Most of the time though, I was shooed away because my arms weren't long enough. Leeah assigned those jobs to Jean and Ruth. When all the flies were trapped in the dining room, that's when Leeah said, "Margaret, open the screen door... quick... open it wider than that."

Leeah and Mae were whipping their rags at a frantic pace now, running from corner to corner. Mama is yelling, "Don't y'all knock over dem lamps... y'all gon brak somethin ef you ain't careful." I'm covering my head trying not to get swatted by those dirty rags and holding wide that screen door until I hear, "Margaret, shut the door... quick! Shut the door!" I shut the door. There are sighs of relief. Whipping out flies is over... until next Saturday.

If Saturday went well enough for Daddy, we could go to the park after church on Sunday. In the beginning, the whole family would go, even Daddy.

Everybody in town was there, Black people, White people, old people, little kids, and families. There was a zoo with caged lions, tigers, bears, zebras, and monkeys. An old, derelict, but smart, Colored couple who were self-proclaimed docents would tell visitors the same one-sentence refrain as they pointed to the monkeys: "Dese monkeys here, dey ain't nothin' but White folks with no clothes on."

There were families and kids screaming in the swimming pool. I went to the pool during the week for free swimming lessons. Lots of Black kids and White kids came including my "cousin" Alana, who was the prettiest Colored girl in town. She was real light skinned and had curly hair. She didn't worry about her hair frizzing up after getting out of the pool.

People would just walk around or sit at picnic tables. Stuff like hamburgers, hotdogs, cotton candy, ice cream, popcorn, and sodas were for sale. We didn't buy anything, since we already ate at home.

In the middle of the park, next to the swings and the sandbox, was a big dance hall. It was a rectangular wooden building surrounded by wooden railings. The building was high off the ground, so it was hard to see inside, but people inside could look over the railings and see out. Loud rock 'n' roll music was always playing on the jukebox. This was the Colored kids hangout. I knew that because the only faces I saw looking over the rails were black faces. White kids must not go in there 'cause I never saw White faces looking over the rails. I didn't know why it was like that. I know we were not allowed to go in there because Daddy didn't believe in dancing and all that "frolicking that don't mean nothing". But my sisters reasoned among themselves that they had to go where all the black kids were in order to make friends. So Leeah, Ruth and Jean started sneaking in the dance hall. I stood outside as the lookout.

There was also an open amphitheater where movies were shown on Friday nights. We didn't have a TV, so this was must-see TV for our whole family, except Junior who "would not be caught dead there," and Daddy who was working nights.

Sometimes the movie sponsors had 'giveaways' to keep people coming. One time the prize was for the tallest man and the tallest woman present. Another time the prize went to the family with the best Halloween costumes.

This time they announced a prize for the family that had 'the most kids present at the movie.' When Mama heard that she knew this was a contest our family could win. She didn't have to worry about us girls and all the babies showing up, it was Junior who was about fifteen years old and who had stated many times that he wanted no part of this "nonsense."

But Mama worked on him all during the week anyway: "All you need to do Junior is jes come fer a li'l whil, den you kin go."

"I don't want to come to no park—and be seen with those folks."

So, Friday night, before we left to see another episode of Red Rider, Mama begged Junior one more time to "Please come 'round 8:30."

When the movie was over and Red Rider had triumphed once again, the announcer started the process of elimination to find the family with the most kids present.

"Git your kids all together. We 'bout ta start countin now. Is there a family here with more than eight kids?"

Mama yelled, "Yes," along with a few other families. We were all standing together among the rows of benches waiting for Junior. Mama kept asking, "Is Jun here yet?"

We kept answering, "I don't see him."

"Is there a family here with more than nine kids?"

Mama yelled, "Yes" along with one other voice.

The announcer continued, "Looks like we down to jes two families in the competition now. I want them two families to come on up front here so we kin see you."

We were still looking around for Junior. Ruth said, "He ain't heah."

The announcer continued, "We are down to only two families now. Come on y'all. Line up over here so we kin count."

We all lined up, as did the other family, who was White. The announcer started counting them first, "What's your last name? Bates? Okay—eight, nine, ten. Ladies and gentlemen, the Bates family has ten kids here tonight. Is there a family here tonight with more than ten kids? We gon see now."

We were still looking around waiting for Junior.

"Now, I'm gone count this family. What's your name? Edwards? Okay—Eight. Nine."

Junior stepped out of the shadows and joined the lineup.

"Ten and eleven—Ladies and gentlemen, we have a winner. The Edwards family has eleveeeeen kids. Let's give them a round of applause. They are our winners."

Mama was beaming. She was so happy, clapping and saying, "We won; we won." Junior made a quick exit.

Everybody showed up, and we were the winners. We were all smiles and happy for Mama's success.

The prize was a plastic picnic set for a family of six.

* * *

"Come on y'all. You gon miss Santa Claus if you don't git in de truck now."

We piled in the back of the truck bundled up in coats, hats and boots and covering ourselves with a layer of blankets. For a lot of kids in Mt. Vernon, Christmas really began when Santa stopped by the lobby of the Chevrolet sales office and handed out brown paper bags of candy. Every child in town with eager faces was lined up outside in the cold to wait a turn to walk into the lobby to receive a bag. My sisters and me were always in that line.

I was scared seeing this White man in a red and white suit, with his long white beard perched on a raised platform loudly proclaiming "Ho, Ho Ho" to me as I extended a hand for a bag. Ruth wasn't scared. She went through the line three times saying, "It's warm in that lobby". I was too scared to go through again. I was sure Santa would recognize me and scold me for being 'naughty'.

It didn't matter how much candy we got, Daddy said we couldn't eat any of it until Christmas day. We did not follow that rule. As soon as we got our bag we feasted on the candy canes, cracker jacks, licorice and a few pieces of hard candy.

Christmas time up North with the cold and snow was something new for us barefoot kids from Mississippi. Our school holiday on 28th Street cut us off from everything, except seeing Santa in the Chevrolet lobby and Christmas programs at church on Sundays. So Daddy drove us down Perkins and into town so we could see Mt. Vernon all lit up.

Red, green and blue lights were flashing from every window, doorframe, and storefront. Shoppers wrapped in heavy coats and neck scarves, and loaded down with bags of Christmases, were rushing past each other in a hurry to get somewhere. Parked cars in Lover's Lane around the courthouse square was filled with white kids huddled together laughing and swaying to the beat of loud music coming from the courthouse speakers. I didn't see any Black kids in Lover's Lane. I didn't see any Black shoppers wrapped in heavy scarves and neck scarves hurrying past each other either. I guess they already shopped.

At our house Christmas began when Daddy and Junior went up the hill, found a 'Christmas' tree and dragged it home. Daddy built a wooden stand around the bottom and placed it right in front of that 'big pitcha winda' so everybody could see it. We draped the branches with lights, ribbons of tinsel and paper snowflakes we made at school. The only things missing were presents.

When Santa was no longer 'real', we didn't get wrapped presents; we didn't get presents at all. So there were no presents under the tree. Things that we needed like shoes or a coat were already in the closet. Daddy said, "Dats yo Christmas gif."

Only the little kids who still believed in Santa Claus got a gift. That gift was usually something too big to wrap, like a bicycle, a tricycle, a red wagon, a toy truck, or two big white dolls.

"If y'all don't go to bed, Santa's gon pit ashes in yo eyes". These scary words from Daddy and Mama made us sprint wide-eyed to bed and avoid peeking from under the covers. But before we headed to bed, we put on the table a shoebox or a plate or a basket with our name displayed so Santa could give each of us "Christmas gifts". Every year, we woke up to the same 'gifts', an orange, an apple, two Brazil nuts, and two pieces of chocolate-covered mound candy with soft, white sugary cream inside, my favorite.

Mama started cooking pies and cakes and ordering coons and frying up chickens about a week before Christmas. Santa had to have a slice of cake when he arrived with the presents and we "gotta hav some pies if he don't lak too merch cake." Mama was in charge of making pies and cakes like she did in Mississippi when friends and neighbors dropped by to say 'Christmas gifts' and to hear her say in return 'help yoself'. In Mt. Vernon, we ate most of the pies and cakes ourselves since not too many friends and neighbors dropped by to say 'Christmas gifts'.

On New Year's Eve, we stood on the front porch to watch multicolored skies and to listen to faint blasts of fireworks in the distance. At midnight, Daddy and Junior went out back with the shotgun and fired off three or four shots into the air. When Ed Hines complained, "Y'all gon kill somebody wit dat shooting", Daddy took the shotgun to the tool shed broke it down and put the pieces in drawers and buckets.

On New Year's Day Mama always cooked black-eyed peas for good luck. I never liked these peas and never ate them. Mama didn't seem to care.

She cared about getting a man to come to our house first thing on New Year's Day. In Mississippi, all kinds of relatives and neighbors showed up at your house looking for company and a good meal and most of them were men. But here in Mt. Vernon, getting a man to show up at our house first thing in the morning had to be planned in advance. Mama said to cousin BB, "Kin you come to the house in the morning? You kin brang us good luck fer the New Year." I always wondered if my cousin counted as a man if he was just fifteen years old?

And, I was never sure if Mama got better luck if the man just showed up or if she got the same luck if he was asked to show up. It didn't matter. Every New Year's, Mama continued to arrange for 'good luck'.

Chapter Thirteen

Uncle Pete

Sundays after church was strolling day for a lot of Colored people in Mt. Vernon who had no interest in spending every Sunday in the park. Women in their Sunday best and men in their shiny brown shoes came out to 28th Street to stroll. We watched them from the corner of the house. It was like a parade.

Strolling day took on real significance when Uncle Pete came to town. I saw Uncle Pete for the first time when I was about five. He had just come out of the army, and he came to visit us wearing green wool pants and a matching green fitted jacket with little badges swinging from the shoulders. He had on a pair of real shiny black shoes. It was hot, so he was holding his green hat in his hand. I had never seen a Colored man in an Army uniform before. He was standing so straight and was smiling all the time. He was the best-looking uncle I had ever seen.

He was from way up north, so he talked sophisticated like Aunt Belle. He was also nice.

One time, I fell on the tarred rocks on 28th Street and scraped the skin off my knee. He fixed my knee, just like he was a doctor. He washed the blood and gravel off and wrapped my knee with a clean rag. I was so glad he did that. If Daddy had to take me to the doctor, he would be so mad, and I would probably get a whooping or something.

At first, Uncle Pete came every year during the summer to be with Grandmother and Big Papa and to see some of the people he had met summers before. After Grandmother died, he kept coming. When he arrived, the word got out and every eligible Colored woman in town made it a point to come to 28th Street and stroll.

They were all dressed up in tight skirts, pumps, and fancy hats. Their pumps were sinking into the mud, and their arms were out like wings to keep them from falling down into the mud and dirt. They were determined to make a good impression and catch Uncle Pete's eye. Sometimes if they didn't see him on the porch, some would stop and ask us hiding kids, "Is your uncle at home?"

Sometimes when he was home, Uncle Pete would come on out, greet the ladies, and join them on a stroll down the dusty road.

One time he came during the summer, when I was eight years old. We were always so happy he came to break up our usual long, hot summer routines.

On this particular day, nothing was different. Daddy was at work, Mama was up cooking, feeding, washing, cleaning, changing diapers. Everybody else was playing outside or hanging out at our cousins' house.

"Mama, how am I gon get to work?" Mae pulled on her curls as she paced back and forth in front of the dining room table.

"You know your daddy ain't here—you can ask Pete, if he can take you."

Mrs. Fannie got Mae a job at the White country club where she worked.

"Uncle Pete don't know where that place is." Mae threw her hands up while looking at the clock ticking on the wall over the door. "I'm goin be late".

Mae worked in the ladies changing room. She handed out towels and kept the room clean.

"Go ast him. You kin tell him where de place is at," Mama's stomach was fat again. She sat heavily into a dining room chair, sniffled, and wiped her nose on the back of her hand. She bent and dragged a basket of beans closer to her feet.

Mae left. A few minutes later she returned, grabbing her pocketbook and a sweater.

"He's coming."

I was standing on the side of the house, watching as Uncle Pete drove up in his long, shiny blue car with windows all rolled down. He stopped in front of the two brick pillars.

He was wearing his brown church hat and smiling.

"You ready?"

Mae ran around the car to the passenger side and opened the door. Mama was standing in the front door.

"Glad you gon take her Pete." Mama was laughing, "She wuz goin have ta walk".

"Naugh." He saw me. "Margaret, you wanna take a ride?"

I came out of hiding, smiling and looking at Mama,

"Go on, jes hurry up 'fore you make Mae late."

I ran to the car, opened the backseat door, and got in.

I didn't know if Mae and Uncle Pete were talking or not. I was just looking out the window at the people and places I had seen before.

We went down by the park past Miss Liz's house. She was already on the porch sitting in her big overstuffed chair with her coffee on one side and her knitting stuff on the other.

We passed Horace Mann School, the shoe factory, the cemetery headstone place, and the railroad tracks. We kept going to 10th Street and turned right and went past the Mennonite fruit and vegetable stand.

After that, I didn't know where we were. I didn't remember ever coming over here. We always went the other way to get to town and go to the big grocery store.

Finally, we got to the Country Club. It was hidden among lots of trees and tall grass. We drove along a really long driveway until we got to a white, low-lying building with a lot of flags waving on top. I smelled chlorine, so I could tell there was a swimming pool real close.

"I get out here," Mae said. She opened the door, stepped out, and closed the door. She stuck her head through the open window.

"Thank you, Uncle Pete." She headed to the gate.

"Do you want me to pick you up?" Uncle Pete yelled to her back.

She turned, whispering loudly, "No, I get a ride with Mrs. Fannie." She disappeared behind the gated wall.

We sat there for a few minutes, just looking at other people arriving at the club. White mothers loaded down with towels, rubber tubes, and bags were helping their kids out of cars. Some kids were laughing, some squealing, and some tippy toeing on the hot concrete. They looked so funny. I didn't wear shoes, and the concrete was never too hot for me. I didn't understand why these White mothers have to go through so much trouble to plan fun stuff for their kids. Mama never planned anything for us. We just went outside and made our own fun.

We watched more mothers in their white shorts, pressed blouses, and sandaled feet corral their cheerful, bright-eyed kids through the club gate and behind the white walls. I told myself I had to remember to ask Mae what those White kids do—.

"You want to sit up front?" Uncle Pete startled me.

"Yessir."

I scooted over to the right-side door, got out, and jumped into the front seat.

Uncle Pete started driving.

I was doing what I was doing coming out here, just looking out the window with the wind blowing warm in my face. Mostly I was seeing farmland and tall yellow grass. Then there was a house or two. Sometimes a country road would cut into the tall grass and fields of daffodils. We passed a few of those roads that seemed to go nowhere. Uncle Pete turned into one.

"Did we come this way?" I asked.

"No, this is another way home." he stated.

"Okay," I thought, "I'll get to see something else besides grass and farms." I kept looking for something new to see, but just more of the same. Then Uncle Pete pulled over to the side of the road and turned off the car.

"Why are we stopping here?" I asked.

He said nothing. He kept looking straight ahead.

I looked around for something to see besides a dirt road and tall grass. I saw nothing and nobody.

So, I asked again, "Why are we stopping?"

I was sitting forward, still looking around when Uncle Pete's big hand grabbed my chest.

My mouth fell open. I slapped at his hand. I was confused.

"What are you doing?" I asked. I moved tight against my door.

He took off his Sunday hat and placed it on the dashboard.

"Why are we stopping? I want to go. What are you doing?" I asked again.

"Nothing," he said.

But he was doing something. He was reaching for my hands. He wrestled both my hands together, so I couldn't hit him. With his other hand, he was pulling up my dress.

I was kicking at him and yelling, "Stop it. Stop it. Uncle Pete. You're my uncle."

He was not listening. He used his elbow to try to clamp down on my feet. But I was still kicking him wherever I could.

I was thinking, *Thank God, I'm wearing bloomers.*

He was trying to put his head down on my chest.

I thought, *What is he trying to do? Is he after my titties? Surely not.*

My titties were like little black-eyed peas!

The car seat was like a bench. He picked me up and pinned me down on the seat. My head was banging against the door, but my feet were kicking him in the face.

I was yelling, "Stop, stop it," and one hand was slapping him on his head.

His hands were tugging at my bloomers. I couldn't do much to fight him off. I weighed about sixty or seventy pounds, and I knew he weighed a lot, maybe two hundred or three hundred pounds. He was breathing real hard. I was kicking, twisting, and wrestling to get him away from me..

I was yelling, "Stop it. Stop it. Get away from me." And then I screamed, "I'm gonna tell Daddy!"

Uncle Pete froze. For a few seconds, he didn't move. Slowly, he took his hands off me, sat up, and just stared straight ahead for about a minute.

I was breathing hard and fast, because I was scared and mad. He was breathing hard and fast too, but I was not sure why. Maybe he was tired 'cause he did not expect a good fight.

I watched him straighten his shirt, put on his hat, and start the car. I straightened up my dress, righted myself into a sitting position, and stared straight ahead. I put one hand on the door handle, just in case I had to make a quick exit. As soon as the car stopped at the two red brick pillars in front of my house, I was out the door.

As I was jumping out Uncle Pete said, "I didn't do nothing." I thought, *You tried. I don't like you any more.*

I didn't tell anybody about Uncle Pete's "playing nasty."

Chapter Fourteen

"Stars Are Born"

To make money, a group of churches decided to work together to put on a talent show and singing contest. It was to be held at the Masonic Temple. That meant it was open to anybody who bought a ticket, not just church folks.

Daddy normally did not allow us to participate in anything that was not at a church or at a school. The Masonic Temple had a reputation for hosting activities that were not always "upstanding." Mrs. Chatman, who was a member of Pavey Chapel and the church fundraising chair, convinced him that our church would benefit and that the community would come out if the Edwards Sisters were on the program.

I didn't know how the rivalry started, but this was a contrived beginning of one between the Arnold Singers and the Edwards Sisters.

The "best young singers in town" label belonged to the Arnold Singers. Their group of three siblings consisted of two girls, Sarah and Liz, and a brother, Bobby, who was the pianist. We heard them sing a few times before, and to me, they were very good.

Liz, the younger girl, looked angry all the time with her "pouty" mouth. Sarah looked content to do her job, which was just to sing. Bobby was said to be a "sissy" because of his expressive hands on the piano and the way he swished his behind when he walked. Nobody seemed to mind. He was an entertainer just like Alfie.

This competition was nothing either of our singing groups promoted. It was the church ladies, especially Mrs. Chatman, who were hoping to raise a lot of money by calling the event a "sing-off." The prize was a free dinner and a write-up in the local *Register News.*

I was eight years old.

Naturally, we prepared for the big night. We decided to sing "He's Mine." Jean's job was to listen to the record and write down the right words to the song. She agreed that she should have that job, because her handwriting was "the best."

With the words, right or wrong, the next step was to work on our performance skills. Leeah, Mae, and Ruth would form a semi-circle, and I would stand in front of them. Leeah and Ruth would snap their fingers and swing their outer arm to the beat.

Mae in the middle, would move her shoulders and hips to the beat. I was to rock back and forth with my hands behind my back.

We decided to wear our "best dresses" which meant we would be very colorful and would "brighten up the place." I was in black and white, Ruth in blue, Leeah in purple, and Mae was in red. Jean decided on green. Aunt Helen gave each of us a two-dollar press and curl.

On the night of the sing-off, Daddy drove us to the hall. Outside and inside was packed with people I had never seen at church before. Some were sitting, some standing, and all noisily gearing up for a sing-off battle.

Jean wanted to put on a show. She wanted everybody to "stop being so stiff and do what I do." She reminded us of that when we were announced and as we took our places on the podium.

Our smiling faces, finger snapping, hip swaying, and heads held high brought down the house even before we started singing. I even had a little sway in my hips.

From the musical introduction to "He's Mine," to our burst of harmony with the opening phrase "I've Got Peace of Mind," Jean was uncontrollable on the piano. She was sometimes elevated off the bench, sometimes directing, and sometimes throwing her head back and reaching falsetto heights we had not heard before.

Her hands were flying all over the keys. She ended the performance with a flurry of runs. She then swept off the bench and joined us in repeated bows before our audience. The audience was on their feet clapping and shouting, "Winners!" "Winners!"

We were all smiles as we walked back to our seats in the midst of 'fans' attempting to touch us or shake our hands. We were cognizant of the fact that we were under Daddy's watchful eyes.

After it was over, we were declared the winners. I don't remember getting a free dinner or a write up in *The Register News.* All I remember was Mrs. Chatman running down the center aisle shouting, "New stars are born."

I also remember Daddy saying, "Y'all git in de car an let's go."

Chapter Fifteen

Fire!

I was nine years old when our house caught on fire. It happened on a Saturday during the summer. I know it was a Saturday because that's the day we got ready for Sunday. It was the day when Mama washed our hair, and made a cake for Sunday's supper. It was the day when Daddy bought groceries, fixed fences, and worked on Aunt Helen's house. It was the day Mae, Leeah and Ruth cleaned the house, whipped out the flies, and hung out clothes. It was the day Jean and I hung around with Mama in the kitchen, waiting to lick the cake mixing spoons.

It was the day we prepared to go to the park on Sunday.

Daddy was up on the hill, working on Aunt Helen's house. Mama was in the kitchen making a vanilla cake. The oil stove had a tray under the burners to catch drippings and crumbs. That day, the oil in the tray caught fire. It was a little fire at first, and Mama tried to smother it with a rag. The fire kept getting bigger and reached for the wall above the stove.

Mama yelled to Ruth, "Go git yo Daddy. Hurry up!"

Mama was swinging at the flames with a wet dishrag. Her yelling became more urgent. "Git yo Daddy. Tell him ta hurry—y'all git outta heah."

By the time Daddy got to the house, the fire was attacking the cabinets.

I was trying to see the fire, but smoke was everywhere.

Daddy emptied the bucket of drinking water on the burning stove. He was running through the dining room to get outside to draw buckets of water from the well. He came back the same way and threw it on the fire in the kitchen.

"Ya'll git outta here—git out de way—Mae, go tell Fannie Mays to call de fire department."

Mae ran.

Daddy kept trying to battle the flames that were now devouring the curtains and leaping out the window.

After about thirty minutes, the siren of the fire truck could be heard in the distance. When a siren was heard in Mt. Vernon, it was a signal for White curiosity seekers, the bored and the firefighter-hopefuls to jump in their cars and pickup trucks and match the speed of the fire truck to get to the scene of the fire. Fires were rare in Mt. Vernon. And most folks didn't get a chance to see a house burn down while at the same time meeting and greeting their friends. Witnessing a house burning was an exciting afternoon for White folks in Mt. Vernon.

Daddy fought with water buckets, until told by the firemen to "vacate the premises." He just started getting us kids together and counting heads to see if all of us were accounted for.

"One, two, three, four, five, six, seven, eight—dere suppose to be nine—somebody missing. Cora Mae who is—?"

"Oh, my God. Dolly is in de house—she sleeping."

Mama was screaming and crying and heading toward the dining room door, but the firemen pulled her back. She continued to scream and flail at the fireman.

"Leeah, go git dat baby—she in de back room. Hurry up—go git dat baby—go thu de girage."

Leeah took off to the garage and returned with a still-sleeping Dolly on her shoulders.

The fireman, with their water hoses and axes, hacked their way through the house, watering down everything whether they needed to or not. When they finally turned off their hoses, the smell of water-soaked 2x4s and 4x6s lingered in the air.

We stood together in the side yard, watching and waiting. We overheard a fireman talking to Daddy: "Too much damage to the walls—ceiling, not safe to stay here."

That meant Daddy had to find places for eleven people to stay. Aunt Erma, with her eyes dancing in every direction, tried to show concern by stirring up trouble:

"Sista, Fannie May is why yo house burned down. She ain't call no fire department! She wonted yo house ta burn down."

Mrs. Fannie was explaining to Daddy her version of what happened.

"I called dem fireman—

I don't know why dey took so long—those peckerwoods knowed I wuz Colored. Dat's why dey wuz so long—dey wonted yo house to burn down."

Daddy said many times, "The Lord giveth and the Lord taketh away."

Jean and I spent two nights with Big Mama's sister, Aunt Mae Liza, and Uncle Ean. After one night, we were begging Mama to let us come stay with her at Big Mama's house. Aunt Liza was old and mean. Yanking and pulling our hair was not the way to braid it. After two days, we all moved back into the little yellow house on 27th Street.

Town folks started giving us lots of stuff like clothes, shoes, canned food, bed sheets, and blankets. They put everything on the porch of our burned house. When we moved to 27th Street, Ruth, Jean and I would go to the house to see what new things had come in. That proved to be hard to determine.

One time as we were nearing the house, we saw Aunt Erma and Sam rummaging through the boxes and bags. Seeing us, they set off running, arms overflowing with scavenged items belonging to us, a family of eleven, who had lost about everything.

Aunt Erma was not to be trusted.

Yet she came to our house to talk to Mama almost every day. The two of them sat in the living room when Daddy was at work and talked about—nothing.

"Dese shi-hea some good greens—if ya put in fatback."

"I use ham hocks. A pig foot is good, too."

"Mama coming this Sunday? Maybe Liza is—churning butter—gon tar the road."

There was a lot of pushing out air through their noses and lips, whispering thoughts that were not said out loud. They both were doing the same thing. I wondered how they learned to do that.

Mama laughed about things now, but she had some bad times with her sister growing up in Mississippi. Everything was blamed on her by Erma and believed by Big Mama. And especially when

Erma ran off and got married. Again, Mama was the guilty one, not Erma. Mama told us the story:

"Erma wuz acting all funny at de two-day church picnic. She wuz laffing and looking all crazy 'bout the eyes. Mama says, 'What's wrong wit chou girl?' And Erma say, 'Nothin.' But yo Big Mama knowed dat Erma wuz always doin stuff an actin all crazy 'round boys. So, wen we found out dat she don run off an got married, I got a whooping. Erma said I knowed she wuz gon run off—I didn't know nothin."

I asked Mama one time, "Did you ever tell Aunt Erma what she did to you?"

Mama said, "No, I neva did."

Chapter Sixteen

New House, Old Rules

The Mt. Vernon city limits stopped at 27th Street. That's why there were sidewalks on 27th Street and not on 28th Street. Before our house burned, Ruth, Jean and I went over to 27th Street to skate. We had an old, rusty pair of metal skates, and we had to remember to bring our shoes, so we could take turns skating. I didn't get much skating time, due to the switching-out time between the three of us. All the White kids had their own skates and they laughed and giggled at us during our switch offs. I didn't like those kids very much. We skated anyway. Now that we were back in that little yellow house, we could walk right up to the street and skate.

With our house burned, and because he had to rebuild, Daddy decided to petition the city to make 28th Street and 29th Street part of the city of Mt. Vernon. His request was granted. That meant that we were now entitled to running water, streetlights, and scheduled road upkeep. It also meant that we had to give up our farm animals. Farm animals like ours were not allowed in the city of Mt. Vernon. That was a big change for me, but the backyard had become less exciting since I started going to school.

Daddy and Big Papa slaughtered the sows and sold the pigs. They sold our cow Lucy as well. One by one, our chickens were served up for Sunday suppers, and RedTop, we suspect, died a natural death from loneliness.

Our garden continued to thrive, but in a reduced space. The front part of the garden was seeded for grass. The back half was the garden. Corn stalks were further back in the garden and in the field between our house and Aunt Helen's house.

By the time Daddy finished rebuilding our house, we were no longer a self-sufficient farm family. We now had to rely on store-bought neck bones, chicken wings, eggs, and buttermilk. We washed clothes in a washing machine on the back porch and the iceman no longer came. We got a Frigidaire. And we killed flies with a "Flit" can.

Daddy was working days now, so he could only work on rebuilding the house in the evenings and on weekends. Sometimes, he would get help from Uncle Jay, but everybody was scared he would have a fit if he worked too hard.

One time, when we were in the courtyard sitting around the picnic table, Uncle Jay fell from his seat to the ground. He was twitching and jerking his arms and legs. We didn't know what to do. I had never seen a fit before.

Daddy acted like he had seen one before and knew what to do. He went to the truck, got some kerosene and a rag and started rubbing the liquid on Uncle Jay's arms, legs, and chest.

After a while, Uncle Jay's body stopped jerking. He opened his eyes and looked at us like he didn't know who we were or where he was. Daddy helped him to a seat. I think he started to remember what happened, because he was holding his head down. He looked like he was sorry and embarrassed.

He still helped Daddy with some of the rebuilding.

When we moved back to our house, Daddy had made a lot of changes. The door to the outside was now accessible from the kitchen. Three more bedrooms had been added. We needed them because Mama had a big stomach again.

Mama didn't like all "this city stuff," so she tried as much as possible to hold onto what she was used to. Our outdoor toilet was still occasionally used, but it mostly became a quiet reading room for me. Mama wanted to keep it "jes in case we need another bathroom." She also kept a "slop jar" in the bathroom for the "li'l childrun" to use. We had "city water," but Mama liked drinking water from the well.

"It tastes better," she said.

In the bathroom, the wash pan for a soap and water sponge bath remained along side a new white sink and a bathtub. In the kitchen, the oil cooking stove was replaced with an electric stove and the potbelly stove was removed and replaced with a new oil heating system. The problem with this new system, for me, was that it required oil. It was another oil stove. Oil had caused our house to catch fire! Why did Daddy get another thing that needed oil?

The new system consisted of a barrel-like tub with a grated metal covering inserted into the floor in the dining room. Smaller grated vents were located in each room throughout the house.

I was so scared of oil. What if there was another fire while everybody was sleeping? I spent the next four years going in and out of sleep. Somebody had to be on guard to sound the alarm, just in case of fire.

* * *

The first things we replaced in the new house were the instruments to accommodate our love of music. We got a record player, new records and, eventually, a new piano.

The fire didn't destroy our piano; it was destroyed by the weather. Mt. Vernon summers usually had skies of beautiful puffy white clouds or skies with nothing but hot sun. Tornadoes and tornado-like winds were rare. I only remember one tornado and that one destroyed a lot of houses on the white side of town. So while Daddy worked to rebuild the inside of the house, he moved the piano to the back porch for safekeeping. Along came tornado-like winds and blew the piano off the porch. It was rendered unplayable after that.

With no piano, Jean had to stop taking piano lessons and we, the Edwards Sisters, had to stop singing at home. When our church learned that our piano had been destroyed, they donated one to us. Jean didn't continue her piano lessons because they were too expensive. But we kept making music at home.

Also destroyed in the fire were our two centerpiece white dolls. Among the rubble, we found only their once-beautiful cherub faces, now smokey black. Their dresses were missing, but they were still wearing that fixed, red-lipped smile.

When we moved from 27th Street back to our "new" house, my sisters stopped doing lot of things we used to do. When they stopped, I stopped, too.

I stopped spending hours in the grass in search of tasty grasses and lucky four-leaf clovers. I no longer rushed outside in the rain, put a nail in the dirt to "watch the devil dance." I didn't lay on my back in the grass, staring at the sky, looking at the puffy white clouds and finding bears, elephants, and cows.

I stopped going up the hill to pick plums and eat until my stomach hurt. I stopped making mud people. I stopped outrunning the shade as it slowly covered the sun. I stopped searching for the perfect piece of colored glass to play hopscotch. I stopped chasing butterflies.

* * *

But Daddy remained the same. He continued to work relentlessly on houses for his relatives. He worked the garden and made repairs to the house. He continued to provide for the family, which he had vowed to do. He continued to restrict my sisters' social interactions with their friends.

Going to the fair or to the fish fry in the park was only allowed if and when Daddy also wanted to go. If my sisters were sitting around or just talking, he would tell them, "Git up and go do somethin an quit settin 'round so much."

He continued to remain silent. We wanted him to talk to us. We wanted him to talk about what we were doing or talk about what he thought about what we were doing. He always said that the house stuff was Mama's job. Maybe he felt that showing he cared about what we were doing was not his job. He never picked up the crying babies. He never hugged us, and the word "love" was never said in our house. He never touched any of us unless we were getting a whooping.

Jean and I used to talk about him, "We're just part of his plan. He's always saying, 'every child is a blessing', but he never really talks to us. And he never says anything good."

"I think he's mad all the time."

"Maybe he's too busy working to think about us."

He worked and worked, and he provided for the family. He was the "driver of the wagon," and we girls were to remain quiet and let him make decisions that he felt were best for us, and for Mama.

He never yelled at us for singing and playing gospel records. He never commented on our singing one way or the other.

All the Black folks in town knew us and would stop and say, "Hi. Y'all sanging at the program on Sunday? I'm coming if ya'll gon sang."

Daddy would just smile.

Our Sunday performance calendar was booked up. We had two or three singing engagements on Sunday afternoon at local churches. We also had scheduled engagements out of town in Kentucky or Tennessee. Daddy would drive us to each engagement without a fuss.

We were offered money for our out-of-town performances. Daddy would always say, "No, thank you."

He would say to us, "God gave you a talent, so you kin share it wit others. You don't need no money fer wat you been given."

One time a gospel group from St. Louis heard us sing and wanted to talk to Daddy about a record deal for us. Daddy told us, before even talking to the people, that he "ain't interested in talking to nobidy 'bout no records."

He did agree to meet with the group leader. We were sitting in the back of the church listening.

Daddy said, "No, my chillun don't sang fer money. Dey don't git no money."

The group leader, Mr. Craig tried to explain, "Brother Edwards, we ain't talking 'bout money. We talking 'bout having these young ladies help spread the word of God all over the country. They can do that if they make a record. All they have to do is—"

Daddy cut Mr. Craig off, "I don't wont no chillun of mine runnin 'round gitting mixed up wit all kinds of peoples. I hears 'bout dis record bisness."

Mr. Craig persists, "Brother Edwards, I don't know who you talking about, but we are in the record business, and your girls would go a long way—"

Daddy was standing up to leave. "Thank you, but my daughters ain't gon be goin to St. Louis talking 'bout making no records."

After Mr. Craig left, and we were driving home, Leeah shouted, "Why can't we make a record? What's wrong with that? You just want us to stay cooped up in the house around y'all all the time. I hate Mt. Vernon."

Daddy was driving fast down Perkins and looking over his right shoulder at Leeah.

"You heard what I said. You ain't gon go running 'round wit dese men talking 'bout no records. You don't know a damn thang 'bout men. I know what men want."

Leeah was not finished. "Y'all always talking about men. We ain't talking about no men. We talking about making records. Are we suppose to just sing for these Mt. Vernon folks?"

Mae, who stuttered, added, "W-we the one wh-who doing the sanging. Why didn't— y-you should ask us i-if we want to make—to make a record? We otta stop sanging all together."

Daddy had no more to say on the subject.
We kept singing.

Chapter Seventeen

Feeding the Spirit & the Preacher

At first, Mt. Vernon was God's country, and Sunday was God's day. All the stores in town were closed, so everybody was either walking to church or driving to church. The doors of the church were open. The only things open besides the church were the park and the homemade ice cream stands.

Sundays was the best day of the week for me. It was the day when there were no whoopings, even if Ruth broke a plate. It was the day when Daddy stopped calling White people "sons of bitches" and "dirty bastards." It was the day when Daddy got up early to polish his shoes instead of yelling and fussing at Mama for no reason. And it was the day when there was levity in mind and spirit.

Mama didn't go to church with us. She didn't go any place except to Big Mama's, Aunt Erma's, and Aunt Helen's house. I think she stayed home because her teeth needed fixing and she had no clothes to wear. Daddy never asked her to go anywhere either.

The different preachers who were assigned to Pavey Chapel

wanted to make sure our family stayed at Pavey Chapel. We were the Edward Sisters now, and other preachers wanted us to belong to their church, so we could sing and help them raise money. It was always about money, and they thought we had money. We were a big family, too, so we filled a lot of pews on Sunday morning. Plus, Daddy could pray better than anybody else in town, and our ministers liked showing him off.

When the Presiding Elder came to our church for a conference, the Reverend called on Daddy: "Brother Edwards, can you please lead us in prayer?"

Then, he sat back and watched the show.

Daddy sat in the front pew, so he knelt on one knee and began to pray.

"Dear God, thank you fer allowin us ta git up dis morning an to start 'nother day."

He started out real slow with words you could understand. Then he started adding "ha" after every few words. "Dis morning, lord, ha! You raised me up, ha! An you-ha, pit my feet-ha, on de ground, ha!"

From the Elder, the Reverend, and the other deacons came a chorus of "Amen" after every word. Daddy was beginning to reach his peak:

"He is my-ha refuge, ha! Amen! And my fortress, ha!"

"Alright."

"Amen."

"And you shall-ha, not-ha, be afraid."

Jean and I were sitting real close to each other, because we knew what was going to happen next, and we had to be ready.

Mrs. Hart was at the piano, playing softly, "Yield not to

Temptation." And just about now, what we knew as going to happen began to happen.

Miss Debbie got the Holy Spirit. She was raising her arms and shouting from her seat,

"Yes, Lord. Yes, Lord".

I gave Jean an elbow jab.

Then Miss Debbie got up, moved into the aisle, staggering like an intoxicated zombie, swinging her arms over her head from side to side, and shouting jibberish.

Another elbow jab.

I asked Mama one time, "What's she saying?"

Mama said, "She speakin in tongue."

I never bothered to have that explained to me.

The ushers knew the routine: Rush in, grab Miss Debbie by her arms, fan her while her body writhes out of her control, and hold onto her as she slithers to the floor.

Miss Debbie was wearing a short, tight blue dress, and one of the ushers was tugging at it to try to keep her fat thighs out of public view.

But with all that body twitching like she is being stung everywhere by a wasp—

Elbow jab. Jab and jab.

"Is that—her girdle or is tha—?"

The piano chords intensified as Daddy's words began to come to a close. "We must-ha, have a-ha, humble spirit. In Jesus name, amen."

The "Amens" and "Alrights" came to a stop. The music continued.

Miss Debbie, twitching modestly, was raised to her feet, her forehead dabbed, and she was escorted on wobbly legs back to her seat.

The Elder had been duly impressed with the Holy Spirit at Pavey on this Sunday morning. My elbow was sore for the next three days.

* * *

Having the preacher come to our house for Sunday supper was one of the most important days of the year, for Daddy. Maybe this was a big deal in Mississippi, but I didn't understand why such a fuss was made about it here in Mt. Vernon. The preacher came, ate a lot of food, and then went home.

The visit from the preacher to our home was one of Daddy's proudest moments. It was an opportunity to show off good cooking and to show off our devoted Christian family as an example of God's blessings and His goodness.

To get ready for the big day, everybody had an assignment. Daddy mowed the grass, picked up and put away garden tools, and put lye down the hole in the outside toilet.

Mama made the menu. We wanted collard greens, but because of the flies, we would have turnip greens instead with ham hocks and okra on top. We would also have mashed potatoes and gravy, potato salad, green beans, cornbread, fried chicken, apple and sweet potato pies, and jugs of Kool-Aid made by anybody besides me.

Daddy said, "Don't let Margaret make de Kool-Aid. She don't pit 'nough sugar in dere. Folks like sugar in dey Kool-Aid."

Leeah and Mae were in charge of washing and drying clothes. Jean did the house cleaning, and I did the ironing. I loved ironing. Everybody was happy about that.

By Saturday evening, the house was sprayed for flies and the cooling fans were in each corner of the front room and the dining room. The good plates were washed, and the table was set for six. By Saturday night, hair was washed and braided, under arms and between-the-legs are wiped, and clothes laid out for Sunday morning.

Early on, Mama didn't go to church. But when she did start, she did not go on preacher-coming-to-supper Sundays.

She stayed home to make sure that the amount and display of food lived up to our reputation. The word was out among the preachers assigned to our church that an invitation to supper at the Edwards home was a highlight of their tenure.

This Sunday was Reverend Williams' turn. He was a new guest to our house, so he got a tour first before coming in for supper. The sun was bearing down, and the Reverend was dripping sweat in a three-piece brown suit, but Daddy had to walk him through the bounty of the garden. He must touch the white picket fence surrounding the big backyard and admire the field of green stalks of corn.

When he saw the table, he was expected to grovel, and he did. He was wringing his hands, wiping sweat from his forehead, and praising God and the family.

"Thank you, Jesus. Sista Edwards, God has so blessed you and your wonderful family—and look at this food—God is plentiful".

All eleven of us were in the dining room, some standing, some sitting, and babies sleeping. Mama was more than smiling; she couldn't stop talking.

"Come on in, Revend Williams. Come on in an make yo'self at home. Set down, we got plenty food—don't wait fer us, jes set down an help yo'self. Willie T, why don't you set over heah? Revend, you set anywhere you wont to. Jean, turn dem fans on."

Reverend Williams was brown skinned and tall with a round belly and a receeding hairline. He was still wiping his forehead as he moved to a chair at the head of the table.

"Let's bow our heads and bless this food," he said.

We all stopped in place. I was hoping this would be short; the food was getting cold.

—to nurish our bodies. Amen."

"Amen."

"Why don't you get confoble, Revend? Take yo coat off. You at home."

Mama was moving around the table, waving a rag to keep leftover flies from getting to the food.

I went to my assigned seat in the kitchen at the small table. Between the noisy fans, plate scraping, and the clanging of knives and forks, I only picked up a few words here and there from the big table.

"Um, um the lord—bless you—best greens. I gotta come—great town."

"Eat—have some—got plenty—sweet potato pie? Your children—blessing—never had—singing for the Lord—God's children."

The Reverend had to get back to St. Louis before dark. "Sista Edwards, I sho did enjoy myself. This was the best food I had in a long time".

"Take some witchu, Revend Williams. Let me fix you a plate."

"No, no, don't do that. I wouldn't mind, though, having a slice of that there sweet potato pie. Then I'm goin get on the road."

Daddy said with pride, "We shor enjoyed havin you come to our home—it's a real blessing."

Chapter Eighteen

The Long Walk Home

"Get your stuff together, you're leaving." These words were coming out of Mr. Rollins mouth, but I didn't see him. I put my yellow number two pencil in the slot at the top of my desk, kept my eyes down, and waited. A shadow covered half my desk and me. It couldn't be my friend Judy, because we are all in fourth grade and not tall enough yet to make long shadows.

Maybe, I thought, *I should explore my surroundings.*

I started by raising my head to see where that shadow was coming from. I heard Mr. Rollins' voice again. This time our eyes met—he was talking to me. He was standing over me.

"Margaret, clear your desk. Get your things. You're leaving."

I didn't ask questions. I did as I was told, but I was thinking, *Why am I leaving? Am I going to the Principal's office?*

The other kids were looking at me, giggling and covering their mouths,

"Ohh. Oooh—what you do?"

"You in trrrrrrrouble."

I couldn't be in trouble. This was only my second day in fourth grade. Nobody got in trouble on their second day.

I was so excited yesterday about going to grade four. I was up early and my dress, the one with the blue flowers and the white sash, was pressed and laid out. Mama braided my hair in two plaits on each side of my head. My peanut butter and jelly sandwich on Wonderbread was packed in a brown paper bag. I just had to wait for the others, Ruth in grade six, Jean in grade five, and my brother Frank in grade two. I had taken that three-mile walk since first grade, but this year was supposed to be special, because "Mr. Rollins is the best teacher."

I didn't have a great first day. Mr. Rollins announced his "dictionary."

I looked up to see Mr. Rollins' head tilted to the side, with a firm look on his face.

"Get your stuff, and let's go—you're going to another school."

I was compliant. With shaky hands, I removed my number two pencil from the slot at the top of my desk and picked up my three sheets of paper, placing each carefully on top of the other.

The other kids were chattering, giggling, and pointing. I was standing, pushing my chair under the desk. Mr. Rollins turned his head to face the class, waving a pointy finger in the air and another to his lips. The class hushed.

With my three pieces of notebook paper, my yellow number two pencil, and my brown paper bag containing my peanut butter and jelly sandwich on white Wonder Bread, I followed Mr. Rollins out of the classroom. I followed, hoping my black-and-white checkered dress was down in the back, and that my bloomers were not showing.

Outside the fourth grade classroom, my sisters, my brother, and my cousins Louise, Gilbert, and Sam, were all milling around. The principal, Mr. Fawler, was out there too. But he was standing down the hall at the exit door.

Ruth was complaining to no one in particular, "Why we have to leave this school? Everybody else is still here."

Louise continued the conversation, "We are just being picked on 'cause we don't live around here. Where we gon go to school?"

Ruth continued, "Just you wait till Daddy hear bout this. We being kicked out of school."

"Good luck to you," were Mr. Fawler's words before he left us.

We walked out the double doors of Washington School for the last time. Mr. Brown, the school janitor and all-round handy man, was holding the doors open for us. He was Janet's grandfather. He eyed us, conjuring up a cautious smile on his scraggly face and managing a "Goodbye, y'all," as we head out into the street.

I picked up bits and pieces of the conversation between Louise and Ruth on our three-mile walk back to 28th Street.

Niggers. Peckerwoods. White school.—Somebody told on us.

Mostly, I just walked and contemplated my surroundings. I had no school to go to. This was my last day walking these streets from Washington School. I wanted to pay attention to what I was going to miss seeing.

I never paid much attention to the row houses where Miss Gladys, our Sunday school teacher, lived, and where my friends Bessie and Juanita lived. They reminded me of Aunt Ethyl's house in Mississippi, from the waterlogged, unpainted planks of siding to the open crawl space under the house. Now, I saw that some of the steps up to each house were broken, missing, and all sagging. I never noticed any of these repair needs before. My view was probably blocked by so many kids playing in the yard, and by grandmas in rocking chairs yelling at the kids from the porch.

Then there was the Masonic Temple, the only place where Colored folks had fancy events like fashion shows, parties, and Sing-offs. It was smaller on the outside than I thought, even though it had two floors. The orange paint was dirty. Or was that just the color of it? It was hard to see the paint at the Sing-off because it was dark outside and there were so many people standing around. Anyway, the building needed a coat of paint.

We walked past our church, Pavey Chapel on the corner of Newby and 12th Street. I had thought the yard was bigger. The steps were high, wide and wrapped around the church entrance. And there were no railings. That's why the ushers were sometimes outside to help old people walk up the steps.

The worst kid in Washington School lived on 12th Street. His name was Barry. He had a bad reputation because he liked to fight, and he liked to make up stories to get other people to fight. One time, he made up a story about Ruth. He told Sarina that Ruth called her "the dumbest girl in class." When Sarina was real mad, Barry made arrangements for the fight to take place after school across from the church.

Ruth never tried to save herself. She was always ready to fight. She had a fight because Sarah called her "a cow girl," and she had a fight because Evelyn said she had "country feet." When the name-calling got her real mad, Ruth was ready to fight, and Barry was ready to make it happen.

On that day, Barry promoted this encounter as a fight

between Ruth, "a goody-goody," and Sarina, "a popular girl." There were little kids and big kids, boys and girls everywhere, in the churchyard, and in the street. They were all yelling, "Fight, fight," and pushing the fighters into each other.

I didn't want to be around a fight, so Jean and I walked on down 12th Street to wait and see what was going to happen. What happened that time was nothing. All of a sudden, everybody started running in all directions. Miss Gladys had worked her way into the crowd and was yelling and waving her arms trying to scatter the spectators.

"Y'all better stop dat fightin'. Git on home 'fo I tell yo parents. If you don't wont no whooping, you git on home—y'all know better den dis."

Twelth Street leads to Perkins, which was the main street all the way down to the park. Only White folks live on Perkins. We walked on the side that had the shoe factory where White folks worked, and past Horace Mann School, where White kids went to school.

Across the street from Horace Mann was the Soda Fountain Shop where the White kids hung out. The music was loud and the girls with swaying brown hair, sat on stools laughing, while others strutted about in their collared dresses. The boys were watching and sipping soda pop from bottles with straws. None of them looked at us when we walked by.

There was nothing else to see on Perkins except little white houses with small porches.

When we were walking on Perkins, we always walked grouped together—no stragglers. That was because of the dogs.

I hated dogs. I could never understand why dogs always

chased Colored people. I never saw dogs chasing White people. So, when we are walking down Perkins, I was on guard, never knowing when a dog was going to start chasing one of us.

One time, it happened when Jean and I were walking home from school. A mangy-looking brown and white dog ran up to us in front of Jack's Filling Station. He was growling and showing his teeth. I kept walking real slow, keeping my head straight, paying no attention to that dog. But Jean started looking scared and screaming and running around me, trying to get away from that dog. That dog was smart. He kept moving closer and closer to Jean, showing more and more teeth.

I said, "Jean stop looking at that dog and stop yelling. Be quiet."

But Jean' eyes were wide; her plaits were sticking out from her head. She didn't listen to me.

She just started running down Perkins with writing paper flying and her book satchel flopping around her legs. She ran up and down steps, past the new laundry mat and Tim's grocery store. That dog was fast at her heels. When Jean reached the end of Perkins, that dog just stopped. He went across the street and laid down under a shade tree in front of Mrs. Liz's house. Jean outran that dog. We didn't see a dog the day we left Washington School.

When we got to Perkins Grocery store and waved to Mrs. Liz, who never left her chair on her screened-in front porch, we were just the city park away from home.

We walked on a footpath through the park, under the big oak trees. Shade, at last. The path had the man-made lake on one side and the White baseball field, just down the hill on Circle Drive. When we turned left at the corner, we were on 28th Street.

My sisters and I walked on down the dirt road to our house.

I was scared. What do we tell Mama? No, what do we tell Daddy? I could see a whooping coming for this. I was only nine years old and already kicked out of school. We walked up the burgundy steps and into the living room.

I didn't know how I was supposed to feel, or what I was supposed to do. If Ruth was mad, I worried. When she was mad, she folded her arms tight across her chest and squished up her face like a dried-up prune. I didn't see any of that.

When we walked into the house in the middle of the day, Mama and Uncle Jay were sitting in the dining room with coffee cups and saucers in their hands. Mama saw us and about dropped her saucer of hot coffee all over her lap.

"Wat y'all doin home from skool so early? Did school let out?"

She with her big belly was sitting with her back against the dining room table, holding the cup and saucer in mid-air. Uncle Jay, with his John Deere cap on, was still sipping.

Ruth spoke for all of us: "That old Mr. Fawler told us we had to leave 'cause we going to a new school."

"New school? What new school?" Mama was getting angry now. "Ain't no new skool 'round heah."

Uncle Jay tried to calm Mama down. "Well, Cora Mae, dere is other schools 'round here. Wes Salem. An dere's one right heah—wat is it?"

"Horace Mann?"

"Yeah, Horace Mann, right there on Perkins—y'all pass it evee day goin ta Washington School."

Ruth replied, "Well, I ain't gon go to no Horace Mann School. Nobody else had to leave. We didn't do nothing."

We were all crowded together in the dining room. I was

still holding my number two pencil and three pieces of notebook paper, looking from Ruth to Mama to Uncle Jay, trying to see if I should be mad.

Ruth was saying, "We should go back and tell Mr. Fawler, we ain't goin to no new school."

Mama said between sips from her saucer, "Y'all jes take off yo skool clothes an wait fer yo Daddy ta git home."

I knew Daddy was going to be so mad. And, he was going to blame some peckerwoods for having something to do with this. He blamed peckerwoods for most bad things that happen to Black folks.

Instead of waiting inside for him to come home, we followed Ruth out to the road to wait for him.

Almost everybody on the street had heard about our being "kicked out of Washington School." They were outside, walking real slow up and down the road and talking real low. Aunt Erma, Louise, Sam, Gilbert, Leeah, and Frank were out there walking. Mama with baby Dolly on her hips came out with Uncle Jay. Miss Fanny came out to see what was going on. Mae was in the house on the phone with her friends.

I was trying to hear what was being said.

"They were the ones to turn you in—Dem poor White trash. Dey ain't your friends."

"You out of school? White folks is still trying to keep Colored folks from gitting a edgication".

I asked Mama, "Who trying to keep us from going to school?"

"Dem White folks—It has ta be dat po Peggy Hines."

"Peggy Hines?" I said. "But why they gon—?"

Jean interrupted, "No wonder Kay ain't coming outside—I'll knock her socks off."

After a while, Jean and I decided to throw rocks into the muddy water in the ditches on both sides of the road.

It was getting dark. Uncle Jay went home, and the Hines never came out of their house. Everybody just went home to eat supper.

On a normal day when we heard Daddy's truck park in the driveway, my sisters scrambled to look busy before he came into the house. They grabbed a broom or a dust rag or sat at the table with a book open, pretending to do homework. He wouldn't yell at my sisters if he saw that they were "doing something."

He never yelled at me for doing nothing.

On this day when he got home, we were just walking around, looking scared. When everybody was eating, and Daddy had settled down at the table with a mouth full of brown beans and cornbread, Jean blurted out, "We can't go to Washington School no mo. The principal told us to go home."

There was a beat of silence in the room among us kids, and Mama. Chewing stopped, fingers for raking together beans and cornbread hung in mid-air. Eyes refused to blink.

Finally, Daddy said, "Y'all goin ta West Salem Skool."

Mama said, "How you know dat, Willie T? Who said dey goin dere?"

"Wat you talking 'bout, Cora Mae? You knowed we didn't sign dem papers. So y'all is goin ta West Salem Skool."

"What papers?—What papers y'all talkin 'bout? Where's West Salem?"

My sisters, with puzzed looks on their faces, were all asking questions at the same time.

Mama started remembering. "You mean dat paper dat ole White lawyer wuz trying to git us to sign? He thought we wuz crazy."

The story of why we are going to West Salem went like this: It was common knowledge that White school leaders were doing everything they could to keep Washington School open for Black kids. They wanted to keep all the other elementary schools for White kids.

A White lawyer who was running for office befriended Daddy and Mama, and said he wanted Daddy to help him with his campaign for City Council. This lawyer was well aware of the NAACP's ongoing complaint that Washington School was a segregated school and should be integrated.

The school board decided to zone all the schools. They put West Salem in Zone One and all the other White elementary schools in Zone Two. Washington School had no zone. The lawyer hoped that his friendship with Mama and Daddy would persuade them to sign the exemption papers so we could continue at Washington School. When they didn't sign the exemption papers, we had to go to the school in our zone, which was West Salem.

Mama continued to remember. "An dat's wen we started gitting nasty letters, mostly from White peoples. Black folks was calling Willie T a 'trouble maker.' De White folks wuz saying thangs like 'Willie wuz born in a corn field.' One of dem White folks throwed a big brick up on de porch, almost breaking our pictha winda."

We listened to Mama and Daddy talk about all that zone stuff, but what about West Salem School.

Ruth asked the questions we all wanted an answer to: "Where is West Salem at?—Is there Black kids over there—Do we go there tomorrow?"

The next day a letter came in the mail.

September 1954
Dear Mr. Edwards,

This letter is to inform you that your children will be starting as new students at West Salem School. We want their entry to our school to be as smooth as possible. The information and guidelines you will need to help your children adjust more smoothly is below. Please follow them carefully:

1. Bus Pickup time: 8:15a.m. Place: At the corner of 28th and Circle Drive (near the softball field).

Bus procedure: Students are to seat themselves in the order that they are picked up. Students picked up first must take seats first, starting in the back of the bus.

Bus Leave School: 3:30 p.m. Drop off place: Same as above

3. Dress code: Dress/pants/play shoes/hat (when needed)

4. Materials: Two pencils, eraser, ruler, pad of paper

5. Lunch: Free

We hope you will follow these guidelines as we look to have a great start on Thursday. If you have any questions, contact Mr. Jenkins.

Sincerely yours.

Bob Jenkins
President West Salem School Board
Daddy and Mama read that letter three or four times. Aunt Erma

came to our house because they got the same letter about Gilbert, Louise, and Sam. We kids read it and listened to it being read.

There were still questions like: "Why we have to be out of school for two days—Why do we have to walk down the hill?—The bus always come pass the house to pick up Paul and Ellen!"

Chapter Nineteen

The Enforcers

Thursday morning finally arrived. We were up early. Everything was prepared the night before, hair braided, dresses ironed, shoes polished, baths taken, and school supplies bagged.

I was a little scared. Going to a white school made me think about some bad stuff that could happen over there, like nobody will talk to me or the boys will hit me.

I only ate a biscuit for breakfast. I put on my pink school dress, greased my legs and arms and waited by the front door for everybody else to get ready. The house was so quiet.

At 8:00 a.m., we walked down the road past Ellen's house and down the hill to the end of the road where we were to wait for the bus.

I was standing with Jean, watching Ruth and Louise. They didn't seem to be scared. They were the same as always, talking and joking around.

"You and me will probably be in the same class. That will be fun".

"The teacher is probably old and wrinkled."

I saw the yellow bus. It was coming round the corner like it was coming from the park. It came slowly to a stop on the corner. The driver extended the stop sign. The door opened to a tall, balding, smiling White man with his belly hanging over his belt. He labored down the steps, holding a clipboard with a blue pencil hanging from a string.

"Hello everybody, I'm Mr. Dodge, the principal of West Salem. I want to welcome y'all."

He took a pair of brown reading glasses out of his white shirt pocket and skillfully hung them on his nose. I was standing with Jean in the back of the pack, wondering why we were standing out in the hot sun. Why couldn't we get on the bus?

"Before we board the bus, let's see who we got here."

Mr. Dodge looked at his clipboard, retrieved the dangling blue number 2 pencil, smiled to himself and scanned our faces.

"Which one of you is Leeah—grade eight?" Leeah raises a finger. "Welcome." *Pencil check.*

"Robert—grade eight?"

Pencil check.

"Ruth and Louise—grade seven? Which one is Ruth?"

He was looking over his glasses turning his large head from face to face. Ruth raised a finger.

"Okay, good."

He pointed at Louise, "Then you must be Louise. Welcome both."

Pencil check.

"Okay, where's Jean—grade five?"

"Here." He smiled at Jean. "Thank you."

Pencil check.

"Moving right along. Let's see. Margaret—grade four."

I copied Jean. "Here."

"Welcome, Margaret."

Pencil check.

He pointed. "You must be Sam—grade three."

Pencil check.

Eddie said nothing.

"And last, but not least, you," pointing again, "must be Frank, and you're in grade two."

Pencil check.

"Okay, so all together, there are eight of y'all. Great."

He took off his glasses, folded them into his shirt pocket and tucked the clipboard with the dangling blue number 2 pencil under his arm. He continued with his welcome, "Before y'all get on the bus, I wanna give you some rules about seating. I know your parents got a letter. We have a lot of kids getting on the bus, so we have to fill up the back of the bus first. So, when y'all get on, you have to move to the back and fill up those seats first. Okay?"

He waited and smiled.

"We can get on the bus now."

He climbed on the bus first and walked to the back.

"Come on now—" One hand beckoned us on, and he chuckled. "You don't want to be late on your first day now, do you?"

Gilbert led; the rest of us followed. Mr. Dodge was squeezed between a row of seats near the back so he could direct each of us where to sit.

"Okay, let's have Gilbert, Leeah, Sam, and Frank sit on this long bench. And let's see—two of y'all sit here, and two sit here."

He pointed to the seats across from each other. We followed his directions. Jean and I sat in the seats on the right side of the isle; Ruth and Louise sat across from us on the left side.

"Alright, everybody?"

He was easing out from his place between the seats and rubbing his thick hands together, as if in prayer.

"So, these are your seats every day when you get on the bus in the morning. And when it's time to go home, you take these same seats. Okay?"

Nobody said anything.

Mr. Dodge trudged down the aisle toward the front of the bus, turned smiling with those praying hands again, and said, "Oh, I forgot to introduce your bus driver. This is Mr. Gram."

I looked toward the seated driver who waved a hand and peered at us in his rearview mirror. When I got on the bus, I noticed his white hair and red face.

I was trying not to think what I was thinking. I wanted to know what Ruth was thinking. I looked across Jean to see what Ruth was doing. She was talking and laughing with Louise. I looked behind at Leeah and the boys on the bench seat. They were sitting up, looking out the windows like they were on a field trip or something.

So, I tried to engage Jean in conversation from my window seat. "Where are the other kids?"

"What other kids?"

"Ellen and Paul, they always ride the bus."

"Maybe they're sick today."

The bus was making its way past the softball field, down 27th Street and onto Fishers Lane.

"Where is this bus going?"

I looked again at Ruth. She was quiet now, staring straight ahead.

The bus stopped and picked up Paul.

"Paul ain't sick," I said to Jean.

I was waiting, and we all were, for Mr. Dodge to tell Paul where to sit. He did not tell Paul where to sit. Paul found a seat up near the front of the bus.

We then headed down 28th Street, past our house and on to Ellen's house up the road from where we got on the bus.

"Ellen ain't sick either," I said to Jean.

Ellen got on, waved to her parents standing in the yard. Mr. Dodge did not tell Ellen where to sit. Ellen found a seat up near the front of the bus.

I really wanted to know what Ruth was thinking now, because I was only nine, and I knew something was not quite right.

The driver then moved on down 28th Street, along the park where there were about six or seven kids waiting to get on the bus. When the bus stopped, Mr. Dodge stood up. He said nothing as the kids took seats as close to the front as possible. Each tried to avert their eyes and not look at us as they entered.

Mr. Dodge stood up for each group that got on the bus and each group followed the same attempt not to notice us as they took seats as close to the front as possible. Mr. Dodge said nothing to each group. Some of the kids squeezed three or four bodies into one seat. It was obvious that no one wanted to take the seats just in front of us. The ride to school was quiet for a bus of thirty kids.

When we turned into the school's parking lot and stopped, the driver opened the doors.

Mr. Dodge again stood and said nothing as the students gathered their books and bags and nosily exited the bus.

I stood up, too. Out the window, I saw a large playground

with big trees, swings, and a slide. There was a tall red brick building with lots of windows. Some little kids were running on the playground and others were swinging and jumping rope. There were some big kids talking and laughing near the open door to the building. Men were standing in the parking lot at their open car doors, looking around like they are waiting for something. Mothers were gathering their children and their books and bags and rushing toward the front of the building. Everybody was White. Everybody was looking toward the bus.

When we stepped off the bus with Mr. Dodge leading the way, the crowd became more congealed. Everybody was looking at us like we were animals in the zoo. They were jostling for a position to get a better look at us eight Black kids standing together behind Mr. Dodge. Some of the older boys didn't try to hide their amusement or their scorn. Someone in the group yelled out "Zoo time," as others snickered. Ruth and Louise seemed composed, their heads up, eyes on the crowd. I was in the middle, shielded from the glares.

Finally, Mr. Dodge turned to the crowd of students. "Okay, everybody. I want you all to go to class, now. You heard the first bell. You don't want to be late. Go on now."

The students slowly began to scatter, some getting in last minute looks, sneers, laughs, and monkey imitations.

Mr. Sledge waited as the students cleared the entrance to the school. We were then alone with Mr. Dodge and a few mothers who cautiously smiled in our direction as they made their way to their cars.

"Welcome to West Salem School."

Mr. Dodge was speaking to us as he wiped his brow and

returned his reading glasses to his nose. He had retrieved his clipboard with that blue pencil hanging from a string.

"So, we have a lot of activities and lots of space for students to play, and we have a sports field on the other side. I know you like sports."

He was spreading one arm in the direction of the playground. "Let's go inside."

We all walked inside to a big open space painted yellow with pictures and banners hanging on the walls.

"My office is over here." He was pointing to a closed door with the words, *Mr. Dodge, Principal* labeled on the door. "I know you don't want to be sent to my office."

He chuckled at something he just said.

We continued to walk and look. He continued to talk and point: The cafeteria, the gym, and the music room.

I felt like we are touring the school to see if we wanted to enroll.

Finally, he said, "Now let's go meet your teachers and see your classrooms."

He referred to his clipboard and found me in the middle of the group.

"Margaret. Your teacher is Miss White. And your classroom is right over here."

I was thinking, *Miss White. What a name for a White teacher!*

We went up five steps, passed two doors, and stop in front of a door that said, "Grade Four—Miss White."

"This is your classroom."

He turned and smiled at me. I smiled back.

He went inside and came out with a brown-haired round lady with big friendly eyes.

"You must be Margaret." *Who else could I be?*

She reached out to shake my hand. I gave her the hand that was not holding my satchel. She shook it enthusiastically.

"Welcome to fourth grade, Margaret. We have lots of fun in our class, and you are going to have a great time, too."

She turned away from me.

"Thank you, Mr. Dodge."

She turned back to me, "Now, Margaret, let's go meet your classmates."

She put a warm hand on my shoulder and guided me into a room full of White girls and White boys sitting tall with their hands clasped on their desks.

They were all looking at me with no-teeth smiles plastered on their faces, like our beautiful white dolls that burned in our house fire.

I was standing up front with both hands tight on the handle of my brown book satchel. There must have been at least fifteen pairs of eyes fixed on me like I was "queen for a day." I may as well take on that role—stand tall, head up, smile.

Miss White was saying, "Class, this is Margaret, our new student. Say 'Hi' to Margaret and 'Welcome.'"

"Hi, Margaret. Welcome."

"Good job, class."

"Now, Margaret, your desk is here."

Miss White was guiding again, with that warm hand,

"Next to Johnna and Karen. They are your buddies for the day. They are going to show you the playground and eat lunch with you."

She was using a sing-song voice now.

"You just ask them anything you have questions about. Okay?"

"Yes, ma'am. Thank you."

I exchanged smiles with Johanna and Karen.

I don't remember much about the rest of the day, but I somehow felt my entry into the class had been too easy. Nobody stared at me or tried not to be too close to me. Everybody seemed like having a Black kid in the class was normal. I think the teacher rehearsed them very well on how to be kind to 'the new Colored girl.'

I wished somebody had rehearsed the seventh and eighth grade boys on how to treat me. Because when I walked in the hallway alone, a small group of boys pointed at me, laughed at me and called me names.

At first, I tried to ignore them. But this one boy in particular went out of his way to walk up to me and say in a quiet whisper, "Hey nigger, get outta here".

I tried walking real close to the walls so he couldn't see me. I always looked straight ahead like our cow Lucy and never gave him eye contact.

Still, I couldn't get away from him. I dreaded walking to the cafeteria or to the bathroom, because I knew I would see that boy.

After two days of this, I decided to tell my cousin Gilbert what the boy was saying to me.

"You, you—jes sho-sho him to me." Gilbert stuttered when he talked. "I-I take c-care of-f him".

The next morning, Gilbert and I were on the lookout for the boy. I pointed him out when he was walking down the hall with two of his friends. Gilbert quickly worked his way over to him, grabbed him by the front of his shirt, and with his friends and me looking on said to the boy, "I-I hear you—you been calling—my cousin names. You—you—b-been doin dat?"

The boy's friends scattered while other students gathered. The boy's eyes started darting in his head like a chicken 'bout to have his neck wrung off. His books fell to the floor.

"I –I ain't said nothin—an don nothin," he lied.

Gilbert lifted one finger with dirt under the nail from the hand not holding the boy's shirt, and pointed it directly between the boy's eyes and said as sternly as possible, " I-if you—you ever say—say—another word t-to my cousin, I'm—I'm g-gon break your—your nose". The boy's breathing was shallow like he couldn't get enough air. Gilbert loosened his grip of the boy's shirt and pushed him away. The boy stumbled back, reached for his books from the floor and slithered away, still eying Gilbert before he turned and ran off. I never saw him in the hallways again. Maybe he transferred.

I was pretty happy at school after that. I liked the kids in my class, and I liked my teacher, Miss White. Turned out, she lived on Perkins and I passed her house everyday when I was walking to and from Washington School. Sometimes, I saw her sitting on the porch, but I didn't know her, and she didn't know me. Neither of us could have imagined that someday we would be in fourth grade class together at West Salem School.

That "first-on-the-bus-sit-in-the-back" rule was not sitting well with my sisters, my cousins, or me. The driver was going in crazy circles in order to seat us in the back of the bus. And Mr. Dodge was the enforcer.

For the first two days of school, he rode the bus to ensure that we were following the rule. He also lined us up after school to ensure that we got on the bus first and took our assigned seats in the back. The White kids sat wherever they wanted, coming to school or going home.

We talked about why we had to sit in the back of the bus. Ruth did most of the talking.

"Is Mr. Dodge crazy? He thinks we gon keep on setting in the back of the bus and say nothing about it? He thinks we don't see the White kids setting anywhere they want to? That man must be crazy."

Daddy started going to National Association for the Advancement of Colored People (NAACP) meetings about three years after we moved to Mt. Vernon. He became friends with Mr. and Mrs. Staples, who were founding members of a chapter in Mt. Vernon. Daddy met the Staples at one of their recruitment meetings at church. They were trying to get Black parents with their kids to come to meetings to talk about segregation in Mt. Vernon, and to help raise money for the national organization.

Mt. Vernon had a few families who were considered leaders in the Black community. These families were longtime residents who, through the churches and through Washington School, had managed to establish an acceptable relationship with the White leadership in town. To have an "outsider" come to town and upend established norms and understandings about race and segregation was antithetical to Mt. Vernon's Black leaders.

Most Blacks, and especially Black teachers, understandably didn't want to participate in any organization that focused on getting rid of segregation, if it pertained to Washington School. They felt that Booker T. Washington School, which opened in 1898, was serving the needs of Black students and their families, and it was also providing jobs for Black teachers. Besides, they argued, when students left Washington School, they entered Casey Jr. High and Mt. Vernon Township High School, both of which were integrated and always had been.

Regardless, Daddy started taking us with him to every NAACP meeting twice a month at the Masonic Temple.

Sometimes, Daddy, Frank, Jean, Ruth, Leeah, me, Mr. and Mrs. Staples and their granddaughter, Ella, were the only ones present.

At the meetings, Mrs. Staples introduced topics focusing on the history of segregation in the U.S., and the Civil Rights movement. We read and talked about the 1954 Supreme Court Decision, Brown vs. Board of Education. So, being told by Mr. Dodge to sit in the back of the school bus did not fit with what we were learning in our NAACP youth meetings.

That Friday was day three of our riding in the back of the bus, and Leeah raised the issue with Daddy.

"Daddy, do y'all know that we walk down the hill to catch the bus, but then the bus come pass our house and pick up Paul and Ellen?"

Daddy answered, "I don't see no bus—I is at werk."

Leeah pressed on, "Well, the letter said that if you get picked up first, you have to go sit in the back of the bus. So, Mr. Dodge tells us to sit in the back."

"Why y'all bein picked up first?" Daddy asked.

Ruth took over. "The White kids say they changed the bus route, so we get picked up first—and we have to sit in the back of the bus. The White kids git to sit anywhere they want to".

Daddy got it then. "Y'all better not be setting in the back of no bus. You git on dat bus and set anywhere you want to jes lak dem White kids."

Daddy had given us permission to break the "first-on-the-bus-sit-in-the-back" rule.

Ruth said, "Starting Monday, we gon sit anywhere we want to on that bus."

On Monday morning, I was nervous and scared. I thought everybody else was too. But we were determined to do what Daddy said. There was not much talking and laughing before the bus arrived. When the doors opened, and with Mr. Gram's eyes on us, Ruth boarded first. She did not go to the back of the bus. None of us went to the back of the bus.

We all took random window seats. Ruth sat in a window seat, four rows back from the front. I sat in a window seat, seven rows back from the front. Number seven was my lucky number.

Mr. Gram, his eyes on us through his rearview mirror, drove away, but yelled from his driver's seat, "Move to the back of the bus. You know the rules."

None of us moved.

I could see his eyes squinting. He stared us down as he turned onto 27th Street and began the straightaway to Fishers Lane to pick up Paul. About a block away from that pickup, he pulled the bus over to the side of the road and cut off the engine.

He pulled himself to his feet, looking feeble and wild about the eyes, his hair lying to one side, covering his hearing aid in his right ear. He started stumbling toward us, waving his arms and shouting,

"I told you to move to the back of the bus."

He looked like a red-faced ghost with the sleeves of his white shirt flaring out, and his too-big white pants hanging loosely about his hips.

"Get up! Move!"

I was looking to Ruth to make a move. She was looking out the window.

Mr. Gram was standing over her now yelling and gesticulating wildly.

"Get up out of this seat. You heard me. Get up."

He grabbed her by the arm and started trying to pull her out of the seat.

"Let's go. You know you can't sit here."

He used both hands, trying to drag her into the aisle.

Ruth was fighting back, slapping at him with one hand and holding onto the back of the seat in front of her with the other. I was three rows back from Ruth, so I could see Mr. Gram's sweaty face, his watery eyes, and his quivering hands.

I felt bad for him. Why did they give an old man a job like trying to make eight Black kids sit in the back of a bus, when they know it was not right? I just didn't want him to fall down dead in front of me.

Leeah and Gilbert didn't feel sorry for him, because they jumped up and ran down the aisle to help Ruth.

I was watching a wrestling match. Gilbert grabbed Mr. Gram by the collar, while Leeah added her strength to help Ruth hold her place in her seat. There was a lot of grunting, flesh-on-flesh slapping sounds,

"Stop it." "Get up. Go to your seats."

I looked around at everybody else to see what they were doing. Louise, Sam, Frank, and Jean were just sitting on the edge of their seats, watching the match.

I saw that Mr. Gram was losing, and he knew it, too.

But before a winner was declared, I quickly got up, holding

my satchel to my chest, and ran to my assigned seat in the back of the bus. Louise, Frank, Jean, and Sam got up one by one, deliberately slow, and took their assigned seats as well.

Mr. Gram was puffing and blowing and breathing deeply as he untangled himself from the grasp of Leeah and Gilbert. He was unsteady on his feet as he rolled up his shirtsleeves, realigned his pants, and ran one hand over his face and the other through his hair. He moved to the aisle, watching us and waiting, trying to get control of his breathing. Gilbert and Leeah stared him down to make sure he had no intention to engage Ruth again. Assured, they move to their assigned seats in the back of the bus.

Ruth returned to looking out the window of her window seat, four rows back from the front. Mr. Gram made his way back to his chair and completed the route, his eyes on us all the way.

Other kids getting on the bus showed some confusion, seeing Ruth in their space. They took seats everywhere else—three or four to a seat to avoid that empty seat next to Ruth.

At school, we followed the usual routine, and at the end of the school day, Mr. Dodge lined us up as usual so we could take our seats in the back of the bus for the trip home. We all sat in our assigned seats, except Ruth. She sat in her window seat, four rows from the front. Mr. Dodge did not try to discourage her, and fellow students avoided sitting next to her.

It was about 5:30 p.m. when Mr. Dodge, Mr. Jenkins, and Mr. Gram showed up at our house to meet with Daddy regarding "an urgent matter."

We were not allowed to be at the meeting, but we knew what it was going to be about. We were able to pick up random pieces of the conversation.

"Ruth not follow—obey rules, assigned seats, policy—"

Daddy's words were clearer: "Not set in back—not Alabama—I told her to—NAACP—put yo hands on her?"

When they left, we asked, "What did they say? Is Ruth still gon ride the bus?"

Daddy's response, "Why y'all didn't say nothin 'bout setting in the back of dat bus? Those damn sons-of-bitches must thought we in Alabama—dey dealing with me. I told dem Ruth an none of y'all gon set in the back of no bus ever agin."

Daddy drove Ruth to school for one day. She was back on the bus the following day, sitting in her window seat, four rows from the front.

A few days later, a letter came addressed to all West Salem parents:

The school bus policy, "first-on-the-bus-sit-in-the-back" is now null and void. All bus riders are allowed to sit in any vacant seat.

* * *

West Salem had lots of activities for students to participate in. The only activities at Washington were Girl Scouts starting in grade two, and a Student Office Assistant position offered in grade six. I joined Scouts, and Ruth tried for the office position. She was not selected.

At West Salem, we had sports days, school plays, and spaghetti dinners. And we had an upper school music class. Every week, grades four to eight met together in the big music room for group singing. We sat by grade on the floor, and each of us was handed a songbook. The teacher, Miss Snodsmith decided on the songs we sang. Sometimes, she played the piano, and sometimes, we sang a capella.

All the songs were new to me. At first, I just followed along trying to learn the tunes. Miss Snodsmith picked songs like "Old Folks at Home," "Oh Susanna," "Yellow Rose of Texas," and "Camptown Races." The other kids knew these songs and belted out the words with feeling and enthusiasm.

"Great singing, class", Miss Snodsmith said. "Next, turn to page six, and let's sing, 'Dixie.' Now class let's turn to page forty-nine, and let's sing 'Old Black Joe'."

The word "Black" caught my attention, and the attention of the other kids in my class. Some of the girls tried unsuccessfully not to look at me, while some of the boys just covered their mouths to stifle a snicker.

I looked at the words of the song. We were supposed to sing a song about some Black man and "cotton fields with his head down low"?

I couldn't see what Ruth was doing. But after school, she told us that the words in "Old Black Joe" were saying bad things about Black people. In the next music class, she wanted the five of us to sing "Old Red Joe" instead of "Old Black Joe."

The next time "Old Black Joe" was on the song list, I was ready, sort of. Since I was by myself in my class, I did sing, "I hear those gentle voices calling, 'Old Red Joe,'" but not loud enough to be heard.

Ruth made up for what I lacked. She sang the "Old Red Joe" lyric at the top of her voice. This brought stares from the other kids, disapproving frowns from Miss Snodsmith, and an appearance by Mr. Dodge. Ruth was told after class that she must sing the songs as written.

At the next music class, "Old Black Joe" was on the song list. Ruth sang as loud as she could "Old Red Joe." Mr. Dodge took to observing Ruth through the crack in the open door. When she saw his eyes, she pointed him out to all around her, as he was trying to disguise his presence.

For the remainder of the year, it was a constant struggle between Ruth's trying to bring sensitivity to the music class's song choices, and Mr. Dodge's determination to keep things the same.

"Old Black Joe" was removed from the song list.

Chapter Twenty

Friendship

My best friends in fourth grade were the twins, Karen and Carol. I don't remember how we became friends, but it probably had something to do with Miss White. She may have rehearsed the kids before I entered the class, but eventually her friendly, accepting, and nonjudgmental manner gave all the kids permission to treat me like they would want to be treated.

Before long, Karen, Carol, and I were inseparable. We were shy at first, taking turns smiling at each other. The twins had long brown hair drawn back off their faces and clipped in the back with a plastic clamp. The color of the clamp always matched their dresses.

I got on the bus before them, so when they get on, the two of them sat together. Soon, I moved tight to the window and all three of us squeezed into one seat.

We got off the bus together and went into the building together. We put our book satchels on our desks and went out to play together. We sought each other out during free time activities in class and during gym time.

We talked incessantly about everything, like, "We picked strawberries yesterday," and, "I like strawberries," and, "Do you like 'um better than Paul?"

And sometimes, we played games like, "Which hand has the blue marble in it?" or "I'm gonna go higher on the swing than you." After school, we squeezed together once again in one seat for the bus ride home.

Eating lunch with the twins was one of our favorite times together. So I feared for our friendship when my parents got a letter in the mail stating, "Children on free lunch will need to either pay the daily rate of $1.25 or bring a bag lunch".

My parents could never afford the $6.25 a day needed to buy lunch for the five of us. So added to our morning routine was making, wrapping, and bagging peanut butter and jelly sandwiches for lunch. The letter continued adding, "Students bringing bag lunches will eat their lunch in a separate room assigned for that purpose". This meant that I could no longer sit with the twins and eat lunch. Instead, the 'bag lunch' kids had to eat in a windowless small room down the hall from the cafeteria. An oversized long brown table with chairs took up most of the space.

I didn't know who else would come in there. When my sisters, Leeah, Ruth, and Jean, came in, I was already there sitting near the door, waiting. I thought Louise, Gilbert and Sam were coming, but Ruth said, "They ain't coming in here. They got money to buy their lunch."

The only White kids to come in were Lennie, in fifth grade and his sister, Pat, in sixth grade. I knew them because they got on the bus at the last stop before we arrived at school. I found both of them to be quiet and shy.

They said "Hi", took seats at the far end of the table, and opened the lid of their tin lunch boxes. They both unwrapped their perfectly squared baloney sandwiches on white bread. I know they were baloney sandwiches because they were cut into triangles and I could see the baloney, yellow cheese and mayonnaise. The mayonnaise oozed out every time they took a bite. Their perfect triangles sure did look good.

I opened my brown paper bag, took out the crunched up wax paper covering my peanut butter and jelly sandwich on white Wonder Bread, unwrapped the paper and took a small bite. Eating lunch in a small quiet room away from my friends was like having no lunchtime. I wondered what the twins were eating and what they were talking about.

When Mr. Dodge stuck his head in the door of that windowless room and said, "You're dismissed!", I rushed out to look for my friends. To my surprise and delight, their smiling faces were waiting for me just outside the door of the 'bag lunch' room. For the rest of the year, they collected me just outside the door.

The twins and I never saw each other or got together outside school. I just looked forward to our time at school. During the summer before our fifth grade year, they moved away. I don't think I was sad that they were gone. For me, I had learned the meaning of friendship, unconditional and reciprocal. I felt that with the twins.

Chapter Twenty-One

Sit-Ins

Daddy wasn't going to let anybody keep him from doing and getting everything he felt he was entitled to. Nobody was better than him, even if he only had a second grade education. He used to say, "Wen a black man starts doin wat White men do, White peoples start paying 'ttention to you." And pay attention to Daddy they did.

It was during these times that I admired Daddy most. He had a unique ability to get things done. He was always building something at our house. He worked his way into the Carpenter's Union and worked on houses for other people. He knew the right people. And the right people knew him. He could get anything he wanted, like credit and loans. The lumberyard people knew who he was, the nursery people knew who he was, as did the head of the Mt. Vernon bank. Mayor Dail was Daddy's go-to person to get approval for the NAACP fund drives, and Mayor Dail was a regular guest at NAACP banquets.

When Daddy bought two properties on 10th Street from Realtor Mayor Dail, he started inviting Daddy to his office to get his thoughts on where the city was headed. He also never missed an opportunity to try to sell Daddy more properties.

I felt Daddy could do no wrong. He couldn't fail at anything. I was like him in many ways so I went along with what he said. He didn't believe in dancing, watching too much television or "frolicking", so I didn't either. My sisters would tease me quite a bit: "You just like Daddy—so old fashion and boring."

And we were out there with him fighting segregation and discrimination. Even though he was always "fighting the system," he never preached hate of White people. And we kids didn't either.

Our NAACP involvement, like church, was a source for good, and a source mostly for getting out of the house. All through my time at West Salem and through high school, we were activists—of sorts. When no other kids would join us, the Edwards kids would be out there anyway.

When students in the Carolinas, Georgia, Alabama, and Tennessee were boycotting, picketing, and sitting-in at lunch counters at Woolworth's Five & Dime stores, we were picketing and sitting-in at Woolworth's Five & Dime lunch counter in Mt. Vernon.

I was sitting-in and walking the picket line at the place where I had taken earrings, back in third grade.

Ruth, Jean, and I did a sit-in once at Ray's Diner on 10th Street across from Woolworth's. This was the kind of place where even if Colored folks could sit at the counter and eat, I'm sure none would want to. It was the only other place in town that had a lunch counter, so we had to have a sit-in there.

It was a sleazy, tight, smoke-filled place that served food to "rednecks with bandanas around their necks," and burly men in overalls who looked like they just got off a tractor.

I was scared of those guys. Plus, I was trying not to fall off that high stool when fat White men strutting at our backs and calling us "little niggas" surrounded us. Somebody threw a firecracker that landed near our feet. I was shaking in my shoes but trying to appear calm. We were talking, smiling, and pretending to ignore the sneering and name-calling going on around us. We sat and endured the taunting for about forty minutes, and then we left.

We also had NAACP Relief Fund events to raise money to send to the national office so they could "continue the fight for the rights of Colored folks." I don't know which fear was worse, sitting-in at a greasy spoon diner among a bunch of rednecks or standing in the crazy traffic on 10th Street, asking for money from drivers in cars, trucks, and buses. It was decided that Ray's Diner was not worth the trouble, but collecting for the Relief Fund was a necessary fear.

Non-NAACP kids joined us in the streets to collect money. Beginning around 7:00 a.m., we would gather at the Masonic Temple, and Mrs. Stakes would go over the words we should use to ask for money. We should smile and say, "Hello, would you like to contribute to the NAACP Relief Fund?"

Then Daddy would review the appropriate demeanor if racial slurs were directed at us. If someone cursed at us or made a racial slur, we were to just walk away instead of saying, "You're a nasty peckerwood" or using some inappropriate gesture. We were nervous, but we were determined to go out with our collection cans, wait at each traffic light, canvas each driver and collect money for a worthy cause.

Our reception from the drivers varied. Sometimes, we got enduring words of encouragement like, "Good luck" or "Here's a ten." At other times, we got discouraging words like, "Get out of the street," or "I don't believe in this stuff."

And from others, racial slurs like, "Niggers, get off the road" or "Go back to Africa." We adhered to our training.

So many kids were running to cars and trucks and buses that we began to feel more courageous. The collecting took on a festive atmosphere. It became "a happening" in town once per year.

Our local NAACP branch had a yearly fundraising gala at the Holiday Inn. The guest speaker was always someone from the regional NAACP office. This was the biggest event sponsored by black people and it brought out Mt. Vernon's White "Who's Who" of government officials. It also brought out the Black leaders who wanted to be seen with the White "Who's Who" of government officials. However, these same Black leaders never wanted to be seen at an NAACP meeting.

The Gala was an opportunity for Black people in Mt. Vernon to dress up and come out to an evening of enlightenment and culture. Ruth especially could dress up, flirt, and hobnob with the elite, all under Daddy's watchful eyes. For Jean and me, we dressed up too, but mostly, we were just happy to be out.

Going to the NAACP National Conventions became our family's vacation destinations. We drove to Minneapolis in 1960, Atlanta in 1962, and Chicago in 1963. When Daddy became president of our local branch in 1959, he and Mama and ten or so of us kids squeezed into our car at the time and drove to the conventions.

Each convention was an adventure. The Chicago trip was

memorable, because that 1959 Dodge "spaceship" had to be junked upon our return home. I never knew what was wrong, but that car was shaking all the way to Chicago and back. I heard the words "shock absorbers," but to me it felt like we were in a horse-drawn buggy, traversing a muddy, potholed road.

Mama would end up staying in the hotel room with the babies, while those of us old enough to attend meetings walked around gawking and trying to see "important people."

We held our breath in Atlanta when Julian Bond smiled and spoke to us once. We just about fainted when he smiled and spoke to us twice. We spotted Roy Wilkins and Dick Gregory in the hotel lobby.

These trips were exciting, but tiring weekends. We got up before dawn and hit the road. I could never explain it, but as soon as we got on the highway, everybody in the car went to sleep, except Daddy and me. I had to stay awake just like I did when we got that new oil heating system in the house. This time, I had to help Daddy stay awake to keep him from falling asleep at the wheel. All kinds of gruesome possibilities entered my mind, like running off the road or running into a big truck or hitting a deer.

So, I engaged Daddy in conversation and tried to get him to talk to me. That was not easy, since he rarely ever talked to me.

On one trip, I asked him, "Why didn't you go to the army in WWII?"

"I didn't have to go 'cause I owned a farm. I come under wat dey called 'specilized on de home front.' I had ta signup ta suppot the war. I had ta raise wat dey told me to raise and dat was soybeans and peanuts. So dats wat we raised."

I showed my appreciation for his engaging in conversation

with me by using encouraging words like, "Wow, I didn't know that," and "That is so interesting."

And I meant that. But I didn't want to push my luck, so I usually ended up singing or helping him read highway signs. Sometimes I asked him what towns we were passing through. It was really annoying that I had to be the one to stay awake in order to save everybody else's life. It should have been a shared responsibility.

Daddy knew what I was trying to do and acknowledged my efforts. "Margaret kept me from falling asleep."

The biggest day for Daddy, our family, and the Mt. Vernon branch of the NAACP was when Daddy went to the March on Washington in August 1963. *The Register News* ran a picture and an article, and Mayor Dail also recognized his participation in the March.

For Daddy, the March on Washington was a personal triumph of "firsts." The March afforded him his first flight, his first trip to Washington D.C., and in his words, "de first time I been wit so many Black an White peoples in one place togetha werkin fer civil rights."

The Mt. Vernon branch of the NAACP had not given up on their efforts to end segregation at Washington School. Under Daddy's leadership, pressure continued on the local school board to adhere to the 1954 Supreme Court decision in Brown vs. Board of Education.

Because of that pressure, the Board gave Black parents a choice. They could continue to send their children to Washington School, or they could send their children to the White school in their neighborhood.

Three years later, Booker T. Washington Elementary School was still segregated. No Black parents wanted to be the first to remove their children from Washington and have them be the first Black children to attend an all-White school in their neighborhood. And the principal and teachers at Washington School were fighting to prevent students from leaving in order to save their jobs.

The NAACP kept the pressure on the Board to desegregate Washington School. They did not want to do that. They did not want White kids going to a Colored school. To prevent that, the Board announced that Washington school was going to close at the end of the year. In 1961, all the Black students started going to the four white schools in the city.

Daddy explained further the problems Washington School faced.

"Dem kids wuzn't learning nothin at Washington School. When dey git ta junior high school, dey flunk everthang. Wen I joined de NAACP, I thought dey wuz goin do wat dey wuz suppose to do—bring dat skool up to standard an integrate dem elementary schools.

"But we didn't know what wuz really going on at Washington School. We come ta find out dat it wuz worst dan in Mississippi. The Black teachers wuzn't paid by de city like de White teachers.

Dey wuz bein paid by left over money from de White teachers. De same thang wuz goin on wit de food; left over food from de White schools wuz brought over an dey give it to de Black kids fer lunch."

"Now you kin tell dat school was not teachin nothin. Only one of de teachers at Washington school was qualified to go teach in a white skool, and dat wuz Annetta Jackson Chavis. None of dem others had a college degree. Dey wuzn't even qualified to be teachers. So dey wuz all out of werk."

The closing of Washington did not endear the Edwards

family to the other Blacks in Mt. Vernon.

* * *

Real friends visited each other. None of us had visiting friends, except Ruth. During her senior year in high school, her White friend, Rebecca, would drive out to the house to visit her. Ruth could never go visit her.

Jean and I did a lot of whispering about the reason for this sudden, fast friendship between Rebecca and Ruth. They were strange bedfellows.

Rebecca was no stranger to us. We knew her from our West Salem days. She was the daughter of Mr. Jenkins, who was involved in the "first-on-the-bus-sit-in-the-back" policy at West Salem School. He was also involved in the suspension of Ruth from the school bus.

Seven years later, his daughter Rebecca was driving out to our house to hang out with her new best friend, Ruth.

We were sure her parents didn't know where she was going and who her "friend" was. These questions didn't seem to matter to the two of them. There was a lot of laughing, whispering, and hand slapping.

Daddy was usually not home to witness these short visits. Even if he were, there would be no objection. Not because Rebecca was White, but because the visits were taking place at our house, under house rules.

Ruth, like Leeah, had to be watched; at least that's what Daddy said. He couldn't watch Ruth all the time, and we knew that Ruth was up to something.

In high school, she talked back to the teachers just like she did at home. And she was sent to the principal's office almost every day. She didn't mind. She wanted to go there. The principal was a good-looking young man, and she flirted with him in her tight skirts and white blouse with the top buttons open.

He sought her out in the hallway and said, "Ruth, come see me at lunch today."

She proudly said to us, "Mr. Kane is always telling me to come to his office. He likes me."

I said, "He is only trying to buy peace. He wants you to stay out of trouble."

Almost every day during lunch, she was in his office.

From all the stares and lustful smiles, I could tell that lots of boys, and men thought Ruth was "stacked." She was not skinny or fat; she was well proportioned and did not shy away from speaking with her eyes, her smile, and her round butt.

The few times we were allowed to walk around in town by ourselves, Ruth always walked real slow in front of the men's clothing store. On cue, this handsome young salesman dressed in the same clothes he was trying to sell would come and stand in front of the store. He and Ruth exchanged looks and smiles, and an occasional, "Hello, how are you?" One time he handed her a note. We never found out what was on that note. But whenever we passed that store, the two of them did not appear to be strangers.

As for Rebecca, it turned out that she liked a Black boy named Jimmy. Ruth was being used as her "excuse friend." In reality, Rebecca was meeting up with Jimmy first and coming to visit Ruth afterward.

It was never clear how involved Ruth was in Rebecca's ploy.

By their graduation day, Rebecca was pregnant with Jimmy's baby. She was hurried out of town to some city in the Midwest. If Daddy found out what happened to Rebecca, he never said anything to Ruth or any of us. He must not have heard because there were no new stay-at-home rules put in place for us.

Chapter Twenty-Two

Picking

It was so hot outside during the summer. Everything had to be done early in the morning before the sun came up.

A couple of times during the month, Mae would say, "Tomorrow, let's go pick blackberries." We didn't have to ask or be told to go. We liked being out there in nature fighting off bees, flies, and bugs. We never saw snakes.

Berry picking was always announced in advance, because it required preparation. We needed the right clothes—a wide hat, a long-sleeved shirt, long pants, boots, or high-topped shoes. And we needed the right equipment—a bucket for the berries, a stick for walking and for pushing back vines and bushes, and a jar of water.

We got up at around 5:00 a.m., dressed, grabbed a biscuit, and headed out. We intended to walk first on the wagon path leading to the pigpen and then along the long wagon path from Fishers Lane all the way past Fatty and Skinny's house. All along these two paths were bushes loaded with berries. I mostly stayed on the wagon paths, picking one berry at a time to keep from getting pricked by the thorns.

"Ouch, oh. That hurt."

Nobody was listening to me. I looked around, but nobody was near me. Everybody was up ahead, off the path and deep into the bushes. Mae, Leeah, and Ruth had their heads down, both hands grabbing berries like a machine—right hand pick, left hand to bucket; left hand pick, right hand to bucket. Jean and I were still holding our bucket in one hand and picking one berry at a time with the other.

One time, Daddy said we needed a lesson in "hard work" so he took Ruth, Jean, and me on a day trip to a farm in Kentucky to pick cotton. He said, "Y'all always talkin 'bout too merch work—you need to see what werk wuz lak wen I wuz yo age in Mississippi."

We dressed like we were going berry picking, only instead of a bucket, we got a long crocus sack with a cloth strap. We were supposed to fill that sack with cotton. All I had to do was bend over in my assigned row, take the cotton from the boll, and put it in the sack.

It looked easy. Daddy was picking from two rows at a time. His back was bent, his sack was over his shoulder like a handbag, and his hands seemed to know where each cotton bulb was. He filled his sack, took it to be weighed, and met us on his way back down picking from two more rows.

"Is that all y'all picked? You gotta pick faster dan dat. You ain't gon make no money."

I tried to pick faster, but the bolls had prickly tops, so I had to be careful. And it was so hot, and I was tired, because I had to get up so early to get down here. Plus, I had to bend over, find the opening in the sack each time, and the rows were so long.

Ruth decided it was easier to take the whole boll with the cotton in it to help fill her sack. When we weighed out after a day's work, and the man emptied her sack, she got yelled at by the owner and by Daddy for having all kinds of stuff in her sack: bolls, sticks, rocks, and whole plants. I don't know if she got any money at all. Jean got $6.00 for her sack; I got $4.00. That was enough for me to buy a fancy blue dress with pink flowers and a white lace collar from Gladstone Department Store.

Picking berries was easier than picking cotton. Plus, we were eating berries as we picked. When our buckets were filled to the brim and our lips were blue, berry picking was over for the day. We found ourselves deep in the bushes past the plum trees, and across the tall grass leading over to the end of Fishers Lane. We headed home with Mae and Leeah way ahead. Ruth, Jean, and I walked past two houses on Fishers Lane before taking the wagon path home.

We didn't know the names of the people who lived in the houses, but we knew they were White. Sometimes, we saw kids playing in the yard of the first house. The other house was some distance down, just at the point where we made our turn onto the wagon path. The house was all closed up, like nobody lived there. But we soon found out that a White man lived there.

That day as we approach the house, we watched the door and the screen door slowly open. A White man appeared in the doorway. I thought he was going to wave to us and say "Hi." Instead, he stood there, buck naked, right in front of us, holding onto his "between the legs."

We stopped walking. I was looking at Ruth and back at the man.

I asked, "Why we stopping?"

"Do you see that?" Ruth whispered.

"Yea, I see that," Jean replies.

"Margaret, stop looking over there!"

"Why's he doing that?" I wanted to know.

"We ain't gon stand here looking at this. Let's go."

Ruth pushed me forward toward the turn. She started running. Jean and I started running and looking back at the doorway. The door was closed.

We stopped to breathe.

"Oo-ee, that man is nasteee." Ruth was laughing and shaking her head.

"What was he doing?" I want to know.

"You saw what he was doing. Why he—he must be crazy. He was just waiting for us to come so he could do that. Old peckerwood."

"What we suppose to do now?" I asked.

"I ain't gon do nothing. And I ain't gon say nothing to nobody bout this," Ruth said.

On future berry picking treks, we made sure to keep up with Leeah and Mae. When we walked past that house, I didn't look at that door as we made our turn onto the wagon path toward home.

Chapter Twenty-Three

Why Are You Here?

My social life revolved around my friends at West Salem. I no longer saw Black kids except Janet and Ellen because they went to Pavey Chapel. We didn't talk very much. If we did, it was about church stuff like choir rehearsal.

Fifth grade had more of an academic focus than grade four. My teacher was Mr. Gregory. All I remember about him was that he wore glasses and loved math. On some days, we focused only on math. And he preferred the kids who were good at math. I was not good at math. I found out also at a sports day track meet that I was not good at running either. The one thing I was good at was singing.

There were very few secrets in Mt. Vernon, whether in the Black community or the White community. Word got around especially if it was about a contest-winning group of singing Black sisters called the Edwards Sisters.

I was not surprised then that I was selected to join the West Salem Singing Ensemble. We were four girls, all fifth graders.

There was one alternate, Pat, who occasionally came to rehearsals.

We practiced with the music teacher, Miss Snodsmith, three mornings a week before school. Most of our performances were across the street from the school at West Salem Episcopal Church. Sometimes, we sang in town at the Women's Club. Other times we represented West Salem School at singing competitions at Mt. Vernon Township High School. Our repertoire consisted mainly of ballads like "Greensleeves" and songs by Burl Ives like "Big Rock Candy Mountain." We sang spirituals like "He's Got the Whole World in His Hands."

"Why are you here?" The question came from my friend Barbara, as I was bending over my desk, putting my books inside.

"What do you mean 'why am I here?'" I replied, closing my desk as I turned to go outside. "I go to school here."

Barbara, her dark hair bouncing, caught up with me.

"Everybody else in your singing group went to Benton," she said. "Why didn't you go?"

I stopped and turned to stare at her.

"They left already?" I asked.

I was trying to think. Did I forget that we had to sing somewhere?

"Pat went in your place 'cause she was—"

I stopped listening to Barbara. I walked down the hall to Miss Snodsmith's room to ask her what was happening.

Some woman I had not seen before told me, "She's not here today."

My eyes were welling up. I couldn't let anybody see that I was upset and confused. Was I deliberately left behind? I walked into the bathroom and sat on a toilet to collect my thoughts.

I concluded that they did not want me to go to Benton. Miss Snoddy Nose did not want a Black girl to be in the group that represented West Salem. She used me. She used my voice to sing around Mt. Vernon but would not let me spend a day out of school on a trip to Benton to sing! She planned all along to take Pat in my place, even though she never came to practice.

The bell rang.

I rose off the toilet, flushed, put my face through a few twists, my mouth through a pushed-out pout and back to a flat line. I walked out of the stall, facing the sink and the wall-to-wall mirror. With the warm water running over my hands, I chose a face with eyes open wide and a casual smile. I left the bathroom. I walked down the hall to my classroom and sat down at my desk. I could feel the eyes of my fellow classmates on me, wondering, "Why are you here?"

When I got home, I didn't say anything to Mama or Daddy. I never said anything to them about my day, and they never asked. They were not involved in my school life like that. Mama was too busy caring for the house and babies. And Daddy was too busy making a living. It was my job "to go to school and get an education." I didn't even tell Jean.

The next day at school, I didn't say anything to Miss Snodsmith either. She found me in the hallway.

"I didn't take you on the trip, Margaret because I was trying to protect you."

I just looked at her and thought, *You lying old buzzard,* but I said, "Thank you, but you didn't tell me about the trip. I wanted to go."

I walked away dissatisfied with her explanation and equally dissatisfied with my response. I saw my going to Benton as an act of charity that would have benefited her, and all the other White kids and teachers who were there. Let me deal with being in the 'line of fire'. I did not want protection.

I continued to attend rehearsals with the ensemble three times a week because I enjoyed singing.

* * *

I got my first boyfriend in fifth grade. His name was George and he was White. He had dark brown hair parted on one side, and he was always smiling. He gave me things like a pencil and a piece of hard candy. He never said he liked me, but it was common knowledge among the girls that, "Margaret and George are going together." George's parents owned a paint store in town. Sometimes when Daddy and I went in there, George was there, and we said "Hi" to each other.

Our relationship was put to the test when our class was going on a bus trip downtown to see a movie. A movie! B.J. had showed me what a movie was like, and I didn't like it. Everybody in class though kept talking about the Grenada theatre and *The Wizard of Oz.* I had never been to a movie theater. I had never seen a movie, except B.J.'s.

There was much whispering and planning among the girls on how to get George and me sitting together on the bus. Some were planning how to get us sitting together in the movie.

Sara and Johanna asked George, "Do you want to sit with Margaret on the bus?"

I was standing in the back of the pack, close enough to hear him say, "I don't know."

For the girls, that was a "Yes."

Turned out, we had assigned seats on the bus.

At the theater, after buying candy and popcorn, we were assigned two rows for our class and no assigned seats.

Sarah and Becky were in charge of seating George and me next to each other. They were nudging me down the aisle, while other girls were pushing George from the other side. He was trying to wiggle his way out of their grasp. We did end up sitting next to each other.

I was waiting for Sarah sitting on my right to tell me what to do next.

"Move closer," she said.

I didn't do that because George was arm wrestling with Paul sitting next to him. I didn't want to get smacked in the face.

Then, the lights went out and the music began. I was looking around to see where that sound was coming from. I was looking at that giant screen in front of the room. For the next two hours, I was transported into another world, a beautiful place, an unbelievable place. I forgot about George. I was over the moon.

But, overall, my first boyfriend experience went really well.

* * *

In grade six, I continued to sing with the ensemble. I continued in Girl Scouts as well. In Scouts, we met after school and did fun things like making bracelets out of dried acorns and going to a campsite and making sloppy joes.

One fun thing in Scouts was when I was selected by the troop leader to carry the American flag down Broadway during the Memorial Day parade. I don't know why I was selected. It was probably because I was the only Black kid in the entire parade.

It was hot, I was sweating, and the flag was heavy. My arms were aching, my smile was anemic, but I refused to give up that flag.

My Scout leader kept asking me, "Margaret, you want some help?"

I said, "No, I can carry it."

With almost everybody in Mt. Vernon, Black and White, lining the street and looking on, I was determined to keep that flag in my control. I felt I was carrying that flag for my people.

The West Salem Scout program always included taking Scouts on an overnight trip to Springfield, Illinois, the state capital, to visit the birthplace of Abraham Lincoln. If this year was any different for the leaders, I didn't sense it. But I must admit, I thought of a haint from the past: The Benton trip. That trip was for a few hours; this trip to Springfield was overnight. I was naturally on guard.

The four Scout leaders and the ten of us Scouts piled into three cars with a change of clothes, pajamas, a toothbrush, and a pillow, wrapped in a bedroll. In Springfield, we visited the monuments and Lincoln's house, ate lunch at a fancy restaurant, and ended the day in the home of a local Scout family.

I don't know what behind the scenes work was done in advance to get the host parents in Springfield to be so accepting of me. It was like when I entered Ms. White's fourth grade class at West Salem. The host parents and little brothers and sisters acted like a Black girl slept at their house every night.

Bedrolls were spread out on the floor. We slept, ate breakfast, loaded up again in cars, and returned to Mt, Vernon. It all seemed so normal until the troop leader dropped me off at home.

She said to Mama, "She did so well. We were so happy to have her along with us."

Did she tell the White parents that their daughters "did so well," and they "were so happy" to have them along? It was a great trip, until then.

Chapter Twenty-Four

Flaws

Before I started junior high, I started to look back and assess my life so far. I wanted to find out if there was a way to do some of the things I felt I had missed out on. I was either too young to do them or by the time it was my turn, it was out of date.

Like, I never climbed the plum tree on the hill.

I never got to pick the songs The Edwards Sisters were going to sing at church.

I never scrubbed clothes on the washboard.

I never had to get up early and hoe grass from around the turnip greens.

I never got a chance to throw that bucket into the well, lean back, pull that thick rope, and bring up cold water from ten feet below.

I never got a chance to put the rubber seal on the Mason jars when Mama was canning the blackberries we brought home.

I never got a chance to whip flies out of the rooms.

I never got a chance to sneak into the dance hall in the park and watch the Black kids dance.

I never got a chance to learn how to drive our truck.

Going forward, I decided that if I wanted to experience life, I had to take responsibility for making things happen for me.

I realized though that with responsibility comes exposing and accepting one's flaws. Having Black skin was a flaw at Washington School. Being Colored was a flaw at West Salem.

I was Black with Colored skin, and I accepted both. I must move on.

I was real clear about some of my other flaws. Like my feet were a flaw. When I walked, one foot pointed northeast and the other foot pointed northwest. It was like I was confused and didn't know which way I was going.

In Washington School, big kids I didn't even know would see me walking and start laughing. They would point at my feet and say, "Why you walk like that? Are you going this way or that way?"

Daddy just called me "Slue Foot."

I realized that there were some things I could change and some things I could not.

I could change my "slue feet." All I had to do was turn each foot toward the center and forge straight ahead. And that's what I did.

Daddy also called me "big nose," like, "Git yo big nosed self in dere an clean up dat filthy room."

I couldn't change my 'big nose."

I looked in the mirror to see if my nose was indeed big. I agreed that at the age of twelve, my nose was too big for my face. Perhaps, my face would get bigger and then my nose would look smaller.

Daddy also called me "bumpy face." My sisters had bumps on

their faces, but they went away. The hope was that mine would go away too. They didn't. Of all my flaws, the most concerning for me were the bumps on my face.

To Daddy, I must have been one ugly child. I used to wonder if he was trying to break me. Was this a test? Why would he want me to feel bad about myself? Did I pass? I never refuted his provocations.

I was about to finish my three years at West Salem where I felt comfortable with my flaws and myself. I knew what to expect from my teachers and the other students, and they knew what to expect from me.

I knew that when we had square dancing in PE, I would be paired with the leftover boy. I also knew that as we held hands through do-si-dos, and swing-your-partners, the boys would use the side of their pants to wipe me off their hands.

We played together, we ate together, and we worked on projects together. We girls giggled at the boys for gazing longingly at the high school girl who glided into our classroom bringing notes for the teacher and leaving behind a trail of Jungle Gardenia perfume.

My parents felt obliged to attend spagetti dinners and saw me as a townsperson in the school's operetta. My class spent many days after school and during school rehearsing songs like, "What a Bore. What a Bore. There's nothing I want in this store."

My West Salem friends and I had three years of shared experiences. I felt comfortable with them.

* * *

When I started junior high school, we got a TV and Daddy had rules about when and what we could watch. School nights were out, and "trash" was out at all times.

So, on weekends when his truck drove away, Mr. Ed was switched off and on came trash, American Bandstand.

Leeah, Ruth and Jean would start dancing all around the front room. There was a lot of gyrating, twisting and frolicking, while I stood by the window as the lookout.

Starting junior high was scary for me. There were so many things I had not done yet. And what about my flaws?

I also had to get used to being around Black kids again.

I decided to focus on things that were good about me, like my "big legs." Almost everybody agreed that my legs were the best looking of all the Black girls in Mt. Vernon. And this was true even when I was six years old. Barry, who at the age of nine was already the boy to "stay away from" would see me and say, "Woo-wee, how you doing, Legs?"

I also had nice hair. Big Mama said, "You shor got a thick head of long hair." When I got the nerve to ask Aunt Helen to press it, I had a hard time keeping people at church from pulling at my curls.

"Girl, you got some pretty hair."

I was also pretty smart. I was not Mr. Rollins' dictionary, but I was Daddy's "little secretary." I would write his checks, make phone calls, and help him figure out house measurements.

I became a walker again when I started junior high. Jean and I followed the same Washington School route, but we turned left at Horace Mann Elementary. We went past the White kids' soda fountain and walked straight up to Casey Junior High.

The building looked like a three-story red brick factory.

On the first day of school, the hallways were filled with noisy greetings, talk, laughter, and hugs. Kids were going up and down stairways and spilling into long crowded hallways. I was being pushed along in a sea of White faces none of whom I recognized. I turned right, climbed the stairs, entered the bathroom on my right and ran into two boys coming out with quizzical looks on their faces. I turned around, avoiding the eyes of onlookers, relieved to be soon lost in the hallway fray again. Not a good start.

Lunchtime had always been a problem for me. It was a problem at Washington School, and it was a problem for me in junior high. Jean was my guide. I hung outside with her in the courtyard, eating a homemade sandwich of peanut butter and jelly on white Wonder Bread. I felt lost.

Most of the other kids hanging out in the courtyard were Black. Jean knew the Black kids from the year before, and she stood with them, walked in the grass with them, and laughed and talked with them. Everybody liked Jean.

I knew the names of most of the Black kids, like Jerri, Essie, Judy, Pat, and Bobby, and I said "Hi" to them in the hallways. So, during these early lunchtimes, I just stayed close to Jean. I was not adjusting well to this new school environment.

One thing I could always rely on was my ability to do well in my classes. I loved my classes, especially History and English because some of my West Salem friends were my classmates. Elena was in math, Joanna was in English, and Paul and Barb were in History. I felt a sense of camaraderie and belonging, to be able to see them and talk to them.

Sitting down at the dining room table at home and doing

my homework was something I looked forward to daily. I wanted math problems; I wanted to outline chapters. I wanted to be on the Honor Roll. And I was.

Seeing our report card was the only part of our schooling that Daddy seemed interested in. He seemed to think that just our going to school everyday was a guarantee that we were learning and would get good grades. Every quarter, he lined us up to review "how ya'll doin in skool."

He couldn't understand why Mae, Leeah, Ruth and Jean got "dese kinda grades in all dese classes. You go to skool everday. You should be studying, 'stead wantin to keep yo feet in de road all de time."

He told Jean, "You should be gitting on de honor roll like Margaret. You need to work harder den you doin."

I felt bad for my sisters for always getting discouraging words from Daddy about their grades. Jean agonized over Daddy's disappointment in her. She tried to get my honor roll strategy from me.

"How do you remember all that stuff in class? I study but I still get a 'C' on the test?"

I just said, "I read and write everything down. That's how I remember."

What I didn't say was that I spend most of my time studying, and not a lot of time always trying to make friends.

* * *

I was on my own when Jean moved into high school. I was dealing with my face and the uncontrollable acne that continued to appear on my forehead, my cheeks, and my nose. And in an effort to "get rid of them," I scratched, popped, squeezed, and picked at every one that appeared. It was a losing battle.

No one ever said a word to me about my face, except Daddy. He was still calling me "bumpy face." I was not bothered by his name-calling. I accepted the fact that acne was one of my flaws I could not change, but could mitigate.

I remind him, "It is called 'acne.'"

"I don't care wat you call it. Your Mama had dem same thangs on her face."

"No, I didn't, Willie T."

"Don't tell me you didn't. I could feel dem thangs ret under yo skin. Dey jes never come out."

So, I inherited my condition from Mama. Why didn't mine stay hidden like hers? That was a question I could not answer.

That's when I decided to ask for help from one of God's representatives on earth, Rev. Oral Roberts.

On his shows, he was always healing people who were blind or who couldn't walk or who had cancer. If he could heal these kinds of afflictions, surely, he could get rid of a few bumps on my face. So, I wrote him a letter.

Dear Rev. Roberts,

My name is Margaret, and I am writing to you because I have acne on my face, and I would like for them to go away. I have seen you heal many people on T.V. I would appreciate it if you would heal my face. Thank you.

Margaret

I carried the folded letter around in my pocket for several days. I didn't have an envelope or a stamp yet. I also had to get

Reverend Robert's address.

Somehow, the letter fell out of my pocket and ended up in Ruth's hands.

"Um, what's this?"

She was smiling and waving the open letter over her head and out of my grabbing reach.

"Give that back to me, Ruth."

I was screaming. She turned her body gleefully and played "keep away" as she read the letter out loud:

"'Dear Reverend Roberts—' You writing to that crazy preacher on TV?"

"None of your business, just give it back."

I was fighting back tears now, but I wouldn't dare let one tear stream down my face. I needed to treat this as a joke. Mama was busying herself, while Jean was enjoying the game. I stopped grabbing. Ruth kept reading. I stood and stared straight at her. I stopped listening.

"'My name is—Margaret Edwards and—heal my face.' You crazy."

Ruth threw the letter toward me. I picked it up, folded it, put it back in my pocket, and left the room.

Chapter Twenty-Five

Rules, Writing & Puberty

One thing Daddy never got good at was managing my sisters. They were having a hard time living under his "stay at home" rules.

What my sisters wanted was to have the freedom to enjoy their friends. Daddy, on the other hand, was more interested in keeping my sisters from "getting in trouble" while under his roof.

Daddy always had his antennae up when Leeah was out of his sight. She refused to follow the rules. When we were allowed, we went to the park together on Sundays. Instead of walking around talking and eating cotton candy with us, Leeah met up with her boyfriend, Alton. They walked around for a while before she ended up sitting in his car at the lake, in lover's lane. Boyfriend rules were clear. Boys must come to the house, and they must "court" in our newly renovated "courting room."

One time, when Daddy saw Leeah getting out of Alton's car, he shouted at her when she got home.

"You trying to ruin this family? I know what men want."

Leeah countered, "I was just sitting at the lake in the park. What's wrong with that? We can't ever go nowhere—can't do nothing but work around here and go to church."

Daddy continued, "You don't know nothin 'bout men—you better not be setting in no car wit dat boy. If you want to talk to him, talk here at de house."

Leeah was waving her arms to make her point. "I'm never going to bring nobody here and sit up here in that room. People think I'm crazy."

Daddy had the last word, "You ain't going to no park no mo."

And that was the end of that. Luckily, the park was no longer the place to go anyway.

Leeah said all along that Alton was not her type. He was real nice, real smart, and real dark, but he had a car. I think Leeah just didn't like the boyfriend rule.

Another time, we were up the hill under the plum tree, picking up and eating plums that had fallen to the ground. Leeah decided she was going to climb the tree to get better, riper plums. There were no rules about climbing trees. I think the rule was: "You better not fall out of a tree."

I don't know how it happened, but Leeah fell out of the tree and busted her knee. She was screaming and crying. We were scared that she had hurt her knee real bad. Daddy was going to be so mad because "She should have sense enough not to fall and hurt herself." And what if she had to go to the doctor?

Leeah threatened to beat us up if we ever told anybody about her fall or her knee. We saw that her knee was swollen and red, and she couldn't stand or straighten out her leg. Ruth and Jean hobbled her home, entered through the back door, and set her up in the bedroom. She kept her mouth shut and stayed out of Daddy's way for the next few days.

Since Jean was my best friend, I expected her to tell me everything about seventh grade. And with Leeah getting in trouble for breaking the rules, I expected her to know how to stay out of trouble.

She told me stuff about Betty and what she told her about David, who she liked, and she talked to him, and he was just so good looking. And she told me about a party she wanted to go to at Alice's house on Friday, and David was going to be there. And we both knew that Daddy was going to say "No," and that she was not going anywhere.

One day, she called me into the kitchen after school: "Look at this."

She started singing and swinging both arms above her head and snapping her fingers to a tune. Her hips were swaying and twisting in the opposite direction, her eyes were closed, and her feet were in line with her arms.

I panicked. Not because she was dancing, but because she was dancing out in the open—in the kitchen, of all places.

I grabbed her arms. "You know your're not suppose to be dancing."

My eyes were dancing between Jean's swaying body and the kitchen door.

"You're gonna get caught."

"I don't care," she said. "Everybody's doing the Twist."

I was so disappointed in her.

* * *

Starting in second grade, I was a "joiner." I was in Scouts, the grade five Ensemble, plays, and choirs. I got out of the house by my participation and involvement in every school activity that the White teachers would let me join. Participating in church was always fine 'cause Daddy saw that as God's work.

In seventh grade, I decided to enter a school sponsored writing contest. The contest was sponsored by the Rotary Club of Mt. Vernon. The prize was a day trip to the state capital in Springfield. I had already been to the capital with the Girl Scouts in sixth grade, but if I won another trip it would be a fun day out of school.

The topic was, "What Does America Mean To Me?"

I am not sure how many students entered the contest, but I talked Jean into entering with me. Our essays made it to the second round. We had to go to the radio station and read our essays into a recorder. I had to tell Mama and Daddy about the contest, since the recording session was scheduled on Monday after school, and we would be late coming home. After stumbling over the words and starting over three or four times, we finally got the recording completed. The winner was to be announced on the radio on Wednesday.

I never listened to the radio. On Wednesday after lunch, the Principal, Mr. Edelmond, called me into his office.

"Margaret, you won the essay contest."

He was reaching for my hand, but both of mine were covering my open mouth.

"Congratulations!" he said.

"I did, oh my goodness."

I was so surprised. I won something. I got congratulatory remarks most of the day from some kids, but mostly from teachers.

I am sure I held my head up a bit higher after this win. I had never won anything before. In first grade, I couldn't win a coloring contest, because my crayons went in different directions, like my feet.

By the time I got home, Mama already knew. Her friends listened to my speech on the radio. My parents responded as I expected them to.

From Mama: "That's nice."

From Daddy: "Dem peckerwoods thought you couldn't win? You go ta school eveyday, you suppos ta know how ta write."

Socially, I was still having a hard time finding my place between my West Salem friends and the Black kids. I was more comfortable with my White friends, but I felt I was supposed to be with the Black kids.

There were about three hundred kids in seventh grade and only twelve were Black: eight girls and four boys. I was the lone Black kid in my core classes like English, algebra, social studies, and science. There were other classes that were just for boys, like shop, and there were classes just for girls, like Home Economics. A girl named Erma and I were the only Blacks in my Home Ec. class. I liked the class because we got to cook and sew.

The teacher was Mrs. Mayor. She had the perfect look for a Home Ec. teacher, round like a sweet potato and wrapped in a cabbage-green dress.

When we cooked, we were in groups of four. In sewing, we were in groups of two. Mrs. Mayor said we were allowed to choose who we wanted to sew with. But when it was my turn to choose, she chose for me.

She said, "Margaret, you will be sewing with Erma."

I, who always followed the rules, and I, who never talked

back, stood up and said to Mrs. Mayor, "I don't want to sew with Erma. I want to choose my own partner."

Mrs. Mayor's eyes shot open as she looked up from her grade book. With controlled anger, she stared at me.

"I said your partner is Erma. This is my— "

I interrupted her. "That's not fair. Everybody else got to choose, why—?"

Mrs. Mayor interrupted me, "You want to go to the Principal's office? Say another word and you are out!" She pointed a sturdy finger toward the classroom door. Her tight lips were quivering now. She fidgeted with her beehive hairdo but continued to stare me down.

Actually, I wasn't afraid to go to the Principal's office. I knew Mr. Edelmond. His daughter Mary was my classmate at West Salem for the past three years. Mary and I were alphabetically tied to each other. He would probably understand that I was right, but he would have to side with the teacher.

Mrs. Mayor continued to try to show her dominance over me.

"This is my classroom, and I make the decisions here."

I sat down in order for her to feel like a winner. I didn't know Erma at all, but I didn't want her to feel bad. It was a fairness issue. So, I turned and smiled at her. She smiled back.

Mrs. Mayor obviously held grudges. She gave me a D– in the sewing unit. I didn't make the honor roll that quarter.

I surprised myself sometimes. I was not always so compliant. I could stand up for myself. I used to say country words like "yes'am" and "no'm" when talking to a teacher. I stopped when kids started laughing at me.

At home and around relatives, I still had to show respect. It was hard trying to navigate these two worlds. I decided that at school, I would answer "yes" or "no" when asked a question. But at home and with relatives, I would answer by restating the question.

Mama asked, "Margaret, did you wash dem bottles?"

I answered, "I washed the bottles."

Or Daddy asked, "Did you pick up dat trash?"

I answered, "I picked up the trash."

Sometimes, I was misunderstood. Mama would ask, "Is you trying to be smart—do you wont me ta slap you cross yo face?"

I would put on my incredulous face and reply, "All I said was, 'I washed the bottles.'"

I think a lot of Black kids envied me, though. They said I was "stuckup;" that I felt I was better than them. I did not feel that way, even though I lived in a big house, was a member of the Edwards Sisters, and could write.

* * *

When it was cold outside, we were allowed during lunch to go to the gym and sit in the bleachers and watch intramural basketball games. All the Black girls sat in a circle around Jerri and talked, but mostly listened. I didn't sit in the circle but found a place nearby.

Jerri asked, "Why you sitting way over there, Margaret? You too good to sit wit' us?"

"No, no room over there," I claimed.

Actually, I did feel a little "better" than some of them. I didn't know what they were talking about most of the time. And they didn't seem to be interested in doing anything besides just sitting, talking and laughing. I was doing things that they were not interested in. So, I didn't have anything to talk with them about.

There were not a lot of activities to participate in, but there were some like intramurals, Girl Scouts, and the Elite Choir.

Some of the Black girls already said, "I would never join and be selling no Girl Scout cookies—that's for White girls." And playing intramurals was out: "I ain't playing no basketball with them lame-ass White girls and get all sweaty and shit."

But singing in the Elite Choir was of interest to them. They just didn't want to tryout themselves.

"You can sing, Margaret. You should tryout."

I intended to tryout anyway, even though I knew the criteria for selection was not going to be based on my singing ability. The selection was always based on "something else." And as expected, the "something else" criterion was used in this case. I was not selected for the Choir. Another year would pass with no Black student in the twenty-member choir. Still, at least I tried, and I would keep trying.

What I was not "better at" than the Black girls was my knowledge of the "facts of life." That was what I wanted to learn from them. And by far, the best teacher was Jerri.

She was a big-boned, tall girl, with big titties and a big behind. She was real loud, too. Everybody said she was "fast," and she didn't seem to care.

"Girl, that man has the best lips... he went down on me... he was like a hungry dog."

Everybody was laughing and banging on their seats and falling over, and Jerri was telling story after story.

"Yeah, she pregnant—'bout three or four months."

Rosilee was talking now, "I'm gon see him again. If he your boyfriend, you can't just keep saying 'no'. So last night I said 'yes'."

I had so many questions about "going down" and "three to four months," but I laughed and nodded my head along with everyone else.

Later on, when I saw Rosilee by herself, I asked her a clarifying question, "How did you feel after you said 'yes' to your boyfriend?"

A dreamy look came to her eyes and she answered, "I felt like a woman."

I nodded, "Okay."

Sex or anything related to reproduction, menstruation, pregnancy, or products related to personal hygiene were never mentioned in our house. With Mama bringing home a baby almost every year, and my sisters having gone through puberty and more, I had a lot of questions. Jean and I talked about everything, but never about sex.

I learned the street version of sex education from Jerri and friends, and the sanitized version from books in my seventh-grade health class.

Chapter Twenty-Six

Ironing, Jergens & "The Long Way"

It was about this time that I started ironing. I always ironed my red shorts and my white blouse or a church shirt or two for Daddy, but ironing was not my job. I didn't have a job. I made ironing my job. I became obsessed with ironing.

I couldn't wait for Saturdays. As soon as the clothes were brought in from the clothesline, my preparation began.

I set up the ironing board in the dining room next to the table. Then, I picked out my favorite things to iron—Daddy's shirts. Mama put starch in them, so they were real stiff. I got a small pan of water, and one at a time, sprinkled each shirt until it was real damp. Then, I rolled the shirt into itself and stuck it into a pillowcase to marinate. Sometimes, that pillowcase was completely full of shirts, pleated skirts, blouses, pants, curtains—anything that needed to be ironed. I start ironing at around one o'clock in the afternoon, and at six o'clock, I was still ironing.

Mama said, "Margaret, you in de way. Take dem clothes off

de table. Nobidy kin eat wit clothes all over de chairs lak dis."

Every Saturday was like that. I was ironing for everybody. I think Daddy liked that. I ironed parts of his shirts that my sisters had ignored before, like the inside of the cuffs and around all the buttons in the front. He never said how he felt about how I ironed them. He never said anything.

It soon became common knowledge in our house that I was a good ironer and that I never said no to any request.

That's when I got my first job: ironing for White folks.

It was a typical young middle-class White family: husband worked, wife stayed home with two kids. The wife needed someone to iron. It was Mama's job at first. She didn't like ironing, so she said, "Margaret, you lak ironing clothes. You kin have dis job if you wont it."

The wife picked me up once a week after school and took me to her house to iron. Everything was set up for me in a bedroom, and for the next hour or so, I ironed shirts, baby clothes, dresses, and table cloths.

When it was time for their dinner, I was invited to sit and eat spaghetti and meatballs with them. One time we had meatloaf and mashed potatoes. At about six or seven o'clock, the husband would drive me home.

After about three weeks, Daddy said to Mama, "I don't wont Margaret working in no peckerwood's house. An dat White man branging her home in his car—you know better den dat. Margaret ain't got no bisness bein in no car wit dat man. She ain't goin dere no mo."

So, my ironing days for White folks were over. But that didn't stop me from ironing at home.

* * *

One time, I asked Daddy to take me to a doctor to get some help with the bumps on my face. I don't know how we found this doctor, but he was located in Carbondale, Illinois. Daddy agreed to take me. That was the way he was with me.

I was hopeful when I met the doctor. He labeled my bumps as "acne." He wanted to know how long I had experienced acne and what my cleansing routine was. He looked at my face through magnifying glasses; he prescribed some topical medicine and gave me a printout of what we discussed. He told me to make another appointment to see him again in a month.

As I was preparing to leave, he asked me, "Do you have a boyfriend?"

"No," I said.

His response was, "That would help."

A boyfriend would help? What was he suggesting? Would he say that to a White girl?

I left angry, deflated, and hurt.

I knew what he was suggesting. He wanted me to say "Yes" like Rosilee did to her boyfriend. White bastard!

Back in the car, Daddy asked me, "What did he say?"

I just said, "He gave me some medicine and told me about some things that would help."

* * *

Singing was the one thing we were allowed to do at home and at almost any time. There were some exceptions. We knew not to be singing when Daddy came home from work. Singing was not considered work. He wanted to see hands-on work like mopping the floor or washing the dishes. Jean could not practice the piano either. She had to "get off dat piana and go do something."

We were allowed to watch TV shows related to singing and talent, because Daddy liked watching these shows also. So *Ted Mack and the Amatuer Hour* was a family favorite. So much so that Jean wrote and got an audition for us. She got back a date and time for us to appear in New York.

We were all jumping up and down.

"We're gonna be on the Ted Mack show, we're gonna be—"

Daddy intervened, "Y'all crazy, you ain't gon be on nothin. What you doin writin 'bout some damn show? You ain't goin nowhere."

And there were the usual mumblings, "We can't do nothing. Everybody else who can sing, their parents would put them on that show. We can win prizes and money and..."

"Where y'all gon git de money ta git ta New York? Y'all jes talkin foolishness."

Okay, nobody had thought of that.

Leeah added, "I know we still wouldn't be allowed to go even if we had the money."

* * *

I continued in Girl Scouts with my West Salem friends throughout junior high. Daddy never had a problem with my going to scouting activities; the word "girl" in the name meant it was an organization for girls only.

At one of our first meetings in seventh grade, I was happy to see that my friend Janet joined. It was nice to have another Black girl in the troop.

The two of us decided to meet after school and walk down the street to the meetings at the city campgrounds. The meetings were once a week.

On our way, we are walking, talking, and eating candy. Janet was loaded down with bags of all kinds of fizzies, Clark bars, M&Ms, Taffy, jawbreakers, and my favorite, PayDays. She also had balloons, bubble gum, and bracelets.

She spilled out all her goodies on the camp tables. All the other girls couldn't wait for Janet to show up every week. Everybody was grabbing handfuls and asking, "Where did you get all this stuff?"

Janet answered, "I bought it."

"You sure are lucky."

Black girls may think Girl Scouts was all about White girls and selling cookies, but I also learned some facts-of-life stuff there, too.

Near the end of grade seven, our troop went for a week to a sleepaway camp just outside of town. We were to work on outdoor skills, like rope tying and setting up tents. Lots of other troops were at the same campsite. Janet didn't go. So, I was the lone Black girl at camp.

After setting up, learning, and practicing our outdoor skills, we prepared for the evening activities. Our outdoor showers were always like a game of 'hide and go seek' with a lot of yelling and screaming, because "there was boys peeking through the fence trying to see us naked."

After a campfire and the roasting of s'mores, we got into

our pajamas and got ready to listen and participate in our nightly conversations about secret things, like boys and sex. The six of us in our cabin were all at different stages of readiness for these kinds of talks.

I was sitting on my lower bunk, listening. Becky was reaching into her bedroll. She pulled out a bottle of Jergens lotion.

"I know that husbands like lotion," she announced.

"They do? Why?" Asked those of us who were not ready for talk about husbands.

Becky continued, rolling her eyes like, "Y'all should know why."

She told us anyway: "Cause husbands like soft thighs. We gotta put lotion on our thighs—here yu'uns can have some of mine."

I didn't understand why we needed to rub lotion on our thighs for our husbands. But I didn't say anything. I didn't want the others to think that Black girls didn't know what lotion was for. So I joined the others, holding out my hand, palm up to get my squirt.

Becky was still explaining, "You have to rub lotion on your thighs every day to keep them soft. 'Cause when your husband is driving, he likes to reach over and rub your thighs. So, you gotta make sure they are soft."

We were watching Becky pull up her pink flowered nightshirt and squirt a blob in her palm. She rubbed both hands together and began gently massaging her thighs, one then the other.

I never saw Daddy reach over and rub Mama's thighs. I would notice that because he would have to reach over me, Frank and the baby to get to her thighs. Or maybe only White husbands rub thighs.

It didn't matter, because Becky seemed to know about these things. For the next few minutes nothing was said. We were all concentrating on thigh rubbing.

After three nights of rubbing, the bottle of Jergens was empty. What do we do now? Becky assured us that our thighs would be okay until we got home. We just need to make sure that our mothers had Jergens. If not, just make sure to add it to the grocery list.

* * *

In junior high, during the second half of seventh grade, Jean worked hard trying to make friends with the Black kids. She wanted to spend more time with them. In order to do that, we had to start taking the long way home. Walking with the Black kids after school was the only time we saw all of them together.

On most days after school, we went straight home following the same route we used in the morning. To take the long way home and spend more time with the Black kids, we walked from the front of the school down to Newby Street, past our church and down streets like Conger and Forest. Most of the Black kids like Ellen, Rosilee, and Janet lived around there, and after talking and laughing near the church for a while they would venture off in different directions to their homes. Jean and I walked on 12th Street toward Perkins with a couple of other kids. We then turned right on Perkins and headed for home.

When we walked into the house after school one day, Daddy was yelling again. There was nothing unusual about that, but this time he was yelling at Jean and me.

"What wuz y'all doin over town after school? You ain't got no damn business goin no where 'cept gitting yo Black asses straight home. Who told you ta go over dere? Mr. Chavis saw you walking wit dem wild kids—you ain't got no business being over dere 'round dat church. From now on, you never go nowhere, 'cept home."

Mr. Chavis was the father of Janet's stepmother and my second grade teacher at Washington school who had hit my knuckles with a ruler even though I had done nothing wrong. Mr. Chavis had moved to Mt. Vernon a few months earlier to live with his daughter and her new family.

He was of short stature, "black as coal" and had shiny, straight hair. His daughter looked nothing like him. He was thought to be a respected asset to our church and community. He taught Sunday school, was an usher, and he kept an eye out for misbehavior among adolescent kids at church, and in the community. When he told Daddy that he saw Jean and me "over town," Daddy believed he was looking out for our best interest.

For some people, the church is the place where you come "to lay your burdens down." And one Sunday, Mrs. Brown, Janet's grandmother, came to church to do just that. She stood before the congregation a beleaguered, pathetic, brokenhearted, wailing figure and revealed what the whole town already knew. Janet was going to have a baby, and Mr. Chavis was the culprit.

When this news broke, the whole Black community was enraged and paralyzed with stunned disbelief. All the pieces of the puzzle began to fit together for me. There was a connection between Janet's bags of candy and Mr. Chavis' need to stop Jean and me from taking the long way home. Our walking and talking with Janet after school was interfering with the block of time he needed to carry out his acts of abuse and deceit.

The entire Black community was alight with condemnation of

Mr. Chavis. He was run out of town on the next Greyhound bus.

I was waiting for Daddy to participate in the condemnation. I was waiting for him to label Mr. Chavis "a depraved bastard," "a son-of-a bitch," and a liar. I was waiting for him to acknowledge to us the "real reason" Mr. Chavis did not want Jean and me to take the long way home.

Instead, he said nothing. I knew he didn't condone Mr. Chavis' behavior. I just wished he had said so. Instead, he tightened the screws on my sisters even more.

Chapter Twenty-Seven

Family Meetings & 'Affairs'

It was after the Brown family tragedy that I decided it was time to start having family meetings. I approached Daddy with my idea. I explained that the meetings would give family members a platform to speak freely and safely regarding any joys or concerns they had. The meetings would also review and update our work and social events calendar. Our meetings would be biweekly .

Daddy didn't say, "No." I guess he was intrigued by the idea.

From my sisters, the idea was met with: "I don't want to meet—nobody going to say nothing—you always trying to talk about stuff."

The meetings were to take place in the dining room at 5:00 p.m. on Sundays. I made up the agenda and posted it on the Frigidaire, which included things like the dishwashing schedule and upcoming events including, parties, church and school activities, and NAACP meetings.

After some reminders, cajoling, begging, and as a last resort, yelling, "The meeting has come to order." Skeptics showed up to see what was going to happen. For latecomers, it was standing room only.

As the Chair, I introduced broad topics such as, "Anything happening at school this week. How is the NAACP youth group participating in the banquet? Any parties coming up that you want to go to?"

Daddy's reply regarding parties as expected was quick and decisive.

"Ain't no use branging up goin ta no parties—you ain't going nowhere—y'all always jes wont ta keep yo feet in de road."

As Chair, I reminded the attendees that "parties" was an item on the agenda, and we would adhere to the agenda.

The best that I can say about our meetings was that we were sitting together and talking as a family. Actually, we were sitting together and mostly listening. Daddy was still the judge of all concerns.

Maybe our family meetings were just not meant to be. At one meeting, which proved to be our last, Leeah used the agenda item "joys and concerns" to bring up the use of the telephone.

She began smiling coyly, turning her body with her arms swinging from side to side. "Daddy, I know who you been calling when Mama goes to work on Saturdays."

Shucks, I was thinking. *What is she going to say?*

I was looking at Daddy. We all were.

Leeah continued, "You tell the operator the same number all the time. Well, I called that number, and a lady answered the phone. She said—"

Daddy cut her off. "You ain't got no damn business around that telephone. You running your damn mouth 'bout something you know nothin about. From now on, you stay outta dat room."

Leeah was sassy, disobedient, and sat in Lover's Lane. She was defiant; she did not play by Daddy's rules. She pushed her glasses up on her nose, looked at Daddy, and mumbled something like, "I know what I heard."

She wove herself through the stunned faces seated in chairs and left the room.

This was not what was supposed to be said at our meetings, under the agenda item "joys and concerns."

There were no more agends items, so as chair, I said, "Meeting adjourned."

Everybody else left behind Leeah, and I was attempting to leave, trying to look anywhere except at Daddy.

Mama just sat, looking straight ahead. I knew she had questions.

Daddy got up and yelled to an empty dining room, "There ain't gon be no mo meetings. Y'all go clean up dat kitchen."

I didn't understand all the implications of what Leeah said about Daddy's phone calls. But after that revelation, the early morning yelling and screaming going on between Mama and Daddy intensified. It happened mostly Friday nights and early Saturday mornings. Sometimes, I lay there trying to understand the substance of the arguments.

I heard from Daddy stuff like: "You never suport me. You don't wont me ta buy nothin."

I heard from Mama stuff like, "I don't know nothin 'bout wat you buying. You don't tell me nothin."

"I don't hav ta tell you everythan—Ain't nobidy gon tell me what to do. I don't care if I jes got a second grade edjucation. Dese peckerwoods own eveythang an Black folks actin like dey still in slavery."

The worst part of this commotion was that Daddy took it all out on my sisters. The directives began.

"Leeah, Ruth, y'all git yo asses out dat bed and clean this house. And I mean, git up ret now an start doin somethin. You ain't gon sleep all day, git up! You go out dere and pull dat grass from 'round dem cabbage."

Voices from within our bedroom: "It's too early. It's just seven o'clock."

"I don't care wat time it is—you got time to do eveythan else you ain't got no bisness doin. Git up an clean up dis house."

I must say that before Leeah's detective work, there was some curious behavior on Daddy's part that Jean and I had observed.

For the first time in our lives, Daddy asked us if we wanted to go to the County Fair—on a Friday night! Never had he asked us to go anywhere on a Friday night, not even to church. He asked us another time as well. We didn't think too much about it, we were just happy to be going somewhere.

When the County Fair came to town, we were always allowed to go. Daddy would drive us there on Saturday afternoons. The whole family would go and walk around, including Daddy, and sometimes Mama. We stayed until seven or eight o'clock at night, and then Daddy would drive us home.

When Daddy asked us to go on a Friday night, we decided to dress alike. We parted our hair down the middle and braided it into two plaits. We wanted to look like American Indians, for some reason. I wore my red shorts and a white blouse.

Each time we went, Daddy parked the truck on some street in the back of the fairgrounds. He told us to meet him back at the truck at 9:30 p.m. We had no money to spend so I just wanted to walk around, look at all the sleazy-looking men and women inviting people to "come see the two-headed man or the living mermaid." Jean's aim was to just walk around and see who was looking at her, and to see if any of her friends were there.

When we approached the area of the truck around 9:25 p.m., each time we noticed a female standing or leaning against the truck. We would wait in the shadows until she disappeared into the night. We would then get in the truck and drive home in silence.

Maybe this "telephone caper" caused Mama to start "coming out." Ever since I could remember, Mama had missing and decaying teeth. For us, that was normal. That was why she always covered her mouth with her hands, and that was why she never went anywhere.

She had been to the dentist before, because she started having toothaches. She was told that all her teeth had to be pulled out. She was also told that there was no need to try to fix her teeth if she planned to have more babies.

"Having babies take all the calcium you need for good teeth," Dr. Jordan had told her. "We will work on getting new teeth when you finish having babies."

So, Mama told Dr. Jordan, "After this next baby, I ain't gon have no mo babies."

Daddy was not too happy about that kind of talk cause he said, "chillun are a blessing."

But Mama got her new teeth, started wearing her hair up in a bun, threw out her baby tops, pulled and stuffed herself into her old, shredded girdle, bought new clothes and started going to church. When Daddy went to buy groceries, Mama got in the truck. She went downtown to the Five & Dime store and bought some stockings and a new girdle. She went to Gladstone's to buy new pumps.

Mama had been homebound for nine or ten years, but when she went out and met people, they liked her and she enjoyed being around new people.

At church, Mama became a 'lady in white' and started enjoying the company of all kinds of church ladies including those with questionable reputations, like the town gossip, Miss Ruthy, and thrice-divorced Miss Lola. They had their heads together, whispering, eyes bulging, covering their mouths, and looking over their shoulders at somebody. It was hard to tell who or what they were looking at. In any case, there was much laughter that turned to smiles that turned to lingering partings.

Daddy didn't like Mama's new friends.

"Why you have ta talk so merch wit dem gossiping, no good women? Dere's plenty decent women at church—y'all talkin nonsense dat don't mean nothin."

Daddy wanted Mama to be friends with women like Miss Betty Leland. The Leland family of four moved into a trailer a cornfield away from Aunt Helen's house. They said they were from Chicago, but they didn't act like city folk. They acted, talked, and dressed like they were from way down south. Mama and Mrs. Betty became good friends.

Mr. Leland was short, dark brown, wore thick bifocals, and was always dressed in blue faded overalls. One buckle was never hooked. He was rarely seen and rarely heard. His blue pickup truck left early morning and was not seen again until night.

Ms. Betty and Mama were a lot alike. Both were tall, light skinned, and real country in their faded print dresses. They spoke a "foreign language" that each understood.

"What dat in yo gar'en?"

"Is dem greens?"

"I ain't cooked dem befor."

"I sho you—first we gon go pick some pok salad".

"Pok salad, wats dat?

"Cora Mae. Dat dere is grass, ain't it?"

"Naw, dis heah is lak greens. It's good wit turnip greens."

"Girl, den you jes pik dem greens."

That's how Mama and Mrs. Betty spent their days, talking greens, rain, kids, gardens, and mosquitoes. The Leland family must have come to Mt. Vernon not to stay. Mama lost her good friend after six months. They said they were going back to Chicago.

Daddy was sorry to see Mrs. Betty go.

* * *

Mama still wanted to know who Daddy was calling when she was at work.

Daddy wanted to know why she was whispering and laughing with "da worst women in Mt. Vernon."

Daddy must have felt he couldn't answer Mama's question, so when we came home from school one day, he had packed up a bag of clothes and left. It was scary, since we didn't know where he was or when he was coming back.

Everyday after school, I asked Mama, "Is Daddy home?"

"No, he ain't back yet."

I must say that in his absence, the atmosphere in the house felt less tense. We all, including Mama, could relax and do nothing without the constant pressure to be productive. Nobody listened for the car and jumped up to start sweeping or washing dishes. We watched "trash" on TV, and we watched from the couch in the front room, too.

I was not worried. I knew Daddy would come back home.

After a week, Daddy came home, saying he went to Minnesota to look for property. He said he was thinking about moving there. We were listening to his descriptions of houses and lakes, and we were looking at him, knowing we were not moving away from Mt. Vernon.

Mama got her break from all of us when Daddy convinced himself that Mama's new friends were trying to fix her up with their friend, Curtis. Daddy accused Mama of "messing around wit dat man." He told her to "pack yo bag—you goin back ta yo Mama." In other words, he was taking her to Big Mama's house, along with the three babies who were still not yet in school.

We all knew Curtis for his church going, his good looks, and his full head of curly black hair.

Mama's friends, Lola and Ruthy had known all along that Daddy was having an "affair," and convinced Mama that she should have one, too.

At church, Jean and I witnessed a lot of sideways smiling between Curtis, Mama, Ruthy, and Lola. After that, we would all pile into the car, and Daddy would drive us home. That was the extent of Mama's affair.

With Mama gone, Daddy was in charge of her jobs. He had to see to the cleaning, getting everybody off to school and cooking. He told my sisters, "Y'all go clean up dat kitchen and wash dem clothes".

"Mae, y'all needs to pick some okra and cook some greens."

On day three of Mama's being at Big Mama's, and on day three of our complaining about Leeah's hard beans and watery greens, and Ruth's even harder and drier cornbread, Daddy agreed to meet with Big Mama and Mama to work out the terms of Mama's return. Big Mama must have told both of them to "stop acting like fools with all dem chillun at home to take care of." She must have asked Daddy, "How is Sista gon be with some man—she got them babies wit her all the time—and dey got doodoo in they diapers? How she gon git anywhere—she can't drive no car? T, you knows better dan to say Cora Mae is wit some man—you oughta be shame of yoself."

Daddy brought Mama home that very evening.

I think Daddy and Mama used their time away from each other to align their behavior with their values. And as a result, we had a period of peace in the house.

Chapter Twenty-Eight

Cake, Parkinson's & Snuff

Sundays was still the day we went to visit Big Mama. She was no longer cooking for company like she used to, but she still had food available in the kitchen. But mostly these days she made cakes, all kinds of cakes. She had become well known among her church members as the "cake lady." She was also known among her church members as a woman "on the prowl."

Big Mama herself said, "I was never meant to live by myself."

Shortly after we moved into our rebuilt house, Big Mama met and married Mr. Henderson, a cake lover and a newcomer to town. He promoted himself as "a man of means," even though he had no job, no relatives in town, and no place to live.

In Big Mama's estimation, he was a "big, handsome man." He was a well-dressed walker in his tan suit, tan shiney shoes, and his fedora sitting on his big, round, clean-shaven head.

He was a Bible-toting man of God, a member of her church, and had a big voice to match his big ideas. Mama called him a "freeloader." He married Big Mama as soon as possible and moved into her house.

On our visits to the house during these times, Mama and Big Mama sat across from each other on the swings, swatting flies and talking about family.

"Have you seen Mae Liza?"

"Naw, she been sick."

Big Mama picked up her Nescafe coffee can and spit a wad of brown stuff into it. She wiped her mouth with the back of her hand.

"I heard from Belle yesterday."

She took a pouch of snuff from her dress pocket. She reached inside and pinched brown leaves between her fingers. She expertly deposited them into her lower lip.

"How she doing?"

Mama was listening and yelling at us near the street, "Y'all kids git out dat road—you gon git hit by a car."

Big Mama continued, "Belle said she planning on coming down this summer."

She picked up her coffee can again, spit into it, wiped her mouth with the back of her hand, and placed the can next to her chair.

"You know she planning on getting married, to somebody—I thank his name is Derick, he seems real nice."

Big Mama and Mama passed the afternoon, with Mama keeping an eye on the kids and traffic, and Big Mama chitchatting about family, dipping snuff, and spitting.

On these visits, Daddy never sat or joined the conversation. He used to when we didn't have a TV. He loved boxing. If Joe Louis or Sugar Ray was going to fight, he loaded up the truck and headed to Big Mama's house to watch the fight on her black and white grainy TV. He entered into a running commentary about every punch.

Now, he came into her living room with the usual greeting, "How y'all doing, Miss Bertha?"

He then left to go sit in the front yard in the shade. Sometimes, Mr. Henderson joined him.

We kids, through junior high and into high school, would sit on the swings or talk with some neighborhood kids on the side of the street. We were not allowed to take a walk around the neighborhood.

After a time, Mr. Henderson's health didn't allow him to be as mobile as before. He began spending most of his time sitting facing the front door in the dark living room, slouched over like a walrus in a too-small straight-backed chair. Coming into the front door meant coming face to face with Mr. Henderson.

It was not possible to escape his gaze or his wide-legged presence. His eyes were on my face, trying to get eye contact. He held that stare. His right hand dangled between his legs. If I dared to look him in the eyes, that right hand attached to what I thought was his fat thigh. I looked away.

At first, I thought he had some kind of disease, like Parkinson's. I moved quickly past him and headed for the kitchen to view the cake offerings for the day.

I asked Jean about "the stare" and the "hand."

"He does that to you, too!"

I was not convinced that his hand action was deliberate. So, Jean and I tried coming into the room together. We got the same lascivious gaze, and that same wayward right hand. If I happened to come in with Mama, that right hand was still. I concluded then that he did not have Parkinson's.

Big Mama must have noticed Mr. Henderson's staring behavior. She instructed him, "Henderson turn around. Turn around and watch TV. Come on. Turn around."

I decided that in spite of what Mr. Henderson's disease was, I liked Big Mama's Sunday cakes. So I used the back door to get me a slice.

* * *

Mt. Vernon was slower these days. Change had come. The County Fair was moved to Du Quoin, Illinois and Santa no longer stopped by the Chevrolet lobby to hand out candy.

The park was no longer the hub of activity for families. The zoo shut down years before, and the animals left. The dance hall was torn down, the food stands disappeared, and the last episode of *The Red Rider* was the end of the Friday night movies. The swimming pool closed for "renovations." The Veterans stopped handing out free fish and watermelon on Memorial Day. The only things left in the park were the playgrounds for kids and a portable stand selling fruity snow cones.

With the park gone, we were in search of other ways to get out of the house besides school and church.

Occasionally, during the summer, Uncle Lester loaded us up in his truck and drove us to a drive-in movie just across Fishers Lane. Some days, reluctantly, Daddy allowed us to pick strawberries on the Freeland Farm, which was across from the park.

Uncle Lester worked there as a butcher, so we were allowed to pick strawberries and make a few dollars. It was much easier than picking cotton or picking blackberries.

Some evenings when the big lights came on at the baseball field, we walked down and sat on the hill across from Ellen's house and watched the white people at the game. I didn't know much about the game; I liked watching the kids and families. It was like a festival down there. All these mothers and fathers lined up, buying popcorn, and the kids trying to eat from a bag and hold a soda pop at the same time. Popcorn was all over the ground and the parents were pointing their fingers at the kids and yelling. We couldn't hear what they said, but we knew those parents were mad. Some families made it to their seats and some others were standing, yelling, waving their hats, and laughing at the guys hitting balls and running.

We laughed at how everybody there was laughing. There were never any Black families there. I bet if we were there, we would also be standing, yelling, waving our hats, and laughing at the guys hitting balls and running. We would like eating popcorn, too.

Chapter Twenty-Nine

The Foreigner

Sometimes we went to our cousins' house for entertainment. That house was so different than ours. Uncle Lester and Aunt Erma were so different than Mama and Daddy. There were no rules in that house. Nobody went to church, even though Uncle Lester was a "preacher" and was always quoting scripture.

One time he had his own church on Perkins and 10th Street. Daddy took us there twice, but none of our cousins were there. He had a congregation of only five people.

We thought Louise was lucky. She had money to spend. She had lots of shoes, the latest clothes, and she could listen to rock and roll records. Plus, she wore makeup.

She also bought magazines with titles like *True Confessions, True Love,* and *Modern Romances.* She read her magazines right out in the open and in front of Aunt Erma, who said nothing. Carol was always there too, lying on the couch with *True Love* propped up on her chest. Everybody was hanging around in their pajamas, reading love stories, eating potato chips, and drinking sodas.

Louise had magazines lying around on the porch and on the coffee table for anybody to take. So, I took a few. I hid them in my bloomers and headed home. I wore bloomers every day now.

I didn't go into the house; I went to the outdoor toilet. There, I read in peace and quiet and read all the stories about love, fights and tears. All of the stories ended with everybody getting back together again.

Most of the time, nobody came to use the toilet, but if they did, I said, "I'll be out in a minute." I made noise tearing and crumbling up pieces of newspaper used for toilet paper and threw that down the toilet hole. I returned the magazines to my bloomers and walked out, heading for the tool shed. That's where I hid the "love" magazines.

The shed had all kinds of stuff in it, like tools and wires hanging on the walls from nails. There were cans on shelves full of screws, bolts, and tacks. Large cans of different colors of paint were sitting under a long table piled with hammers, measuring tapes, sandpaper, empty jars, and paintbrushes wrapped in newspaper.

One time, when I was looking for a hiding place, I found an old, tattered book stuck in the back of a drawer. I didn't know how it got there. Somebody named Zora Neal Hurston wrote it. It was called, *Their Eyes Were Watching God.* On the inside was a picture of a Black woman.

I asked out loud to myself, "A Black woman wrote a book?"

I had never heard of a Black woman writing anything. I read stories at school about Fredrick Douglass, but we didn't have any books in our house, except encyclopedias. I had never even read a whole book.

Their Eyes Were Watching God was the first book I ever read. I didn't hide to read it in the outside toilet. I read it in the backyard and in the dining room. Everybody could see me reading. And Daddy never told me to "put that book down and do something." If he had, I would tell him that reading is doing something.

By the time I started high school, I was reading whatever I could get my hands on, including *The Mt.Vernon Register News.* That's where I saw this announcement:

"Host Families Needed for Visiting Foreign Students."

A foreign student! I got so excited about the possibility of having a foreign student in our house!

I approached Daddy immediately and told him we should have one at our house. He didn't say "No," he only listened. So I made calls and set everything up. We were to meet and pick up our assigned "foreign student" at the White country club. This pickup location did cause me some concern, but not enough to want to forfeit an opportunity to have a foreign student stay at our house.

Our main responsibilities as a host family were to provide transportation to and from the Club, and to provide a bed for two nights, Friday and Saturday. Everything else was provided by the sponsoring organization.

I got Jean to help me clean the house, especially the bathroom. We made up the twin beds in the middle room with clean sheets and the new blue company bedspreads. I told my siblings to try to act 'intellgent' and "don't do crazy stuff" cause foreigners aren't used to that.

When we arrived at the Country Club, it was *déjà vu* all over again, like when we dropped Mae off to work a few years before. Lots of White mothers and families flitting about in front of their cars, excited to collect their "foreigner." In my case, nobody could drive our car except Daddy, so he was waiting in the car with Jean. I was standing in front of our car, waiting.

Like my first day of school at West Salem, I was the only Black face and the object of "glad to have you" smiles. From some, I got curiosity stares and whispers. I didn't mind all that. I was looking for and waiting near our car to collect our foreigner, just the way they all were.

I see some White girls standing in front of the Club door. That couldn't be them. Then one by one, the foreign students were introduced to their student host.

"Raylan from Chile, your student host is Pam Mills."

Cheers and smiles accompanied Pam as she rushed in to greet Raylan, tugging at a suitcase as they exited from center stage to a waiting car.

I was still looking for a foreigner when I heard, "Bella from Argentina, your student host is Margaret Edwards."

Obligatory cheers and rubbernecking accompanied me as I feigned joy at seeing a thin, White girl in a pink tank top and jean shorts. At first sight, I hated her. She was not foreign. Where was her headdress, her clogs, her sari, her nappy hair, her salwar chemise, or her long black braids? I wanted a foreigner. This girl looked like white girls I see every day! I wanted a girl who was untainted by American culture and prejudices. I wanted a girl who was going to be curious about me, a Black girl, and I about her—"a foreigner."

We exchanged pleasantries in the car, and I asked her about her trip and her family. When we got home, I saw faces peeking out the window trying to get a glimpse of the "foreigner". When we got in the house, everybody had disappeared. I guess they didn't see what I had promised.

I told Bella she would sleep in what I considered "our fancy middle bedroom with the twin beds, double French doors, and frilly white curtains." She did not seem impressed. She didn't grovel like Reverend Williams. We drove her back to the Club for her evening activities.

While Bella was away enjoying her friends at the Club, I looked up Argentina in our encyclopedia. I learned that Argentina, along with Uruguay and Paraguay, were known as the "White" countries in South America. That made things clearer to me. Bella probably never saw or talked to a Black person in her country, and absolutely never spent a night with one in their home.

I thought Bella hated that she was not living with a familiar White host. If she were, her White hosts would accompany her to the Club and participate with her in all the Club activities: tennis, swimming, lunches, and games.

We were not members of the club; no Blacks were. All we could do was drop Bella off and pick her up. She and I slept in the twin beds in the same room, but we had nothing much to talk about.

We were both glad this cultural exchange lasted only two nights. I learned something. I learned that being Black in Argentina and other parts of South America was a flaw, and that was no different than being Black in America.

I wonder what she learned.

Chapter Thirty

The 'Boyfriend' Rule

When I was in grade ten, I had a boyfriend named Steve. Jean was in grade eleven, and she had a boyfriend named Will. Steve and Will were best friends and cousins. Steve was real dark like Daddy, small framed, and smiled all the time. Will was dark skinned, tall, and stout, and had a lisp. It was hard to say that these boys were our boyfriends. We didn't know what that meant. We liked the boys "just as friends," and it was nice to be able to say, "I have a boyfriend".

To placate Daddy, we followed the "boyfriend rule." Jean invited the boys to the house, and we sat for a while in the "courting room." We never called the room by that name. That would be too embarrassing.

This room used to be Mama and Daddy's bedroom before the fire. When the three new bedrooms were added, they moved to the bedroom on the other side of the living room. So, the "courting room" was created for "sitting with gentlemen guests" and other 'important visitors'.

It had what Daddy said were the latest decorating trends, like knotty pine walls and textured ceilings. There were two green couches facing each other and a tall bookcase against the wall displaying our Britannia Encyclopedias. There were family pictures and fancy bowls on a long, low, brown chest in front of the two windows with frilly white curtains.

The room had no door, just a large square opening. When Mama or Daddy walked by, they could see the boys sitting on one couch and Jean and I sitting on the other. Sometimes our little sisters and brothers walked or crawled by or just decided to come in and sit with us. Most of the time I would take them back to Mama. Other times, we smiled and played with them, including engaging with them in baby talk. It was a nice distraction, and the boys found this entertaining.

After sitting for a while, we could leave. We were obliged to go into the front yard and allow our 'boyfriends' to acknowledge Daddy, who would be sitting in the shade of the weeping willow tree, reading his Bible.

With "Good-bye, Mr. Edwards" said, and Daddy's, "Y'all have a good day" response, we were allowed to walk with them to the park. We would spend the next hour in the park, walking around, spooning fruit-flavored ice from a snow cone, which was the only thing left to buy in the park.

For me, Steve was my rebound 'friend.' My first real boyfriend, and love, was Roland, who I met in ninth grade. It all ended with Roland and me when Ruth saw my letter to him and announced her viewing at the supper table.

"Margaret got a boyfriend. She was writing him a letter. I saw it."

Daddy looked up at me from his plate of cabbage, okra, and cornbread.

"You better not have no boyfriend, and you better not be writin him no letter."

I hated Ruth. But I hated myself more for always following rules.

* * *

My friend Lizzy and I were selected to be youth delegates to a three-day church conference in Peoria, Illinois. I was so happy to be going on a trip where all the young people would be Black. Jean was so surprised that I could go, and that I was sent off without a lecture.

"Why do you get to go places, and I can't go anywhere?"

My response was, "You can't go anywhere because you ask, and you want to go to places where boys are—you should join school stuff."

Daddy never stopped me from going anywhere. Like I said, if it was school related or church related, I would just announce where I needed to go. He would not respond, which in essence meant, "Yes, you can go." I think he let me go places also because I made the honor roll.

At the conference, there were delegates from churches in Peoria and from other cities in the region. Two handsome young men, Randel (tall, dark and quiet) and Roland (athletic, dark, and outgoing) were among the delegates.

It was love at first sight for Lizzie and Randel. It was love at first sight for Roland and me. The four of us were staring at each other in the first "meet and greet."

We introduced ourselves and became inseparable. We sat together, walked together, snacked together, and talked together.

When Roland left my side to go home for dinner, I longed for his return, breathless and filled up with love. I didn't need food; I couldn't eat. I had no appetite. The other kids understood,

"I know you in love, but are you gon eat your fries? If you don't want'em, I'll take em."

On day two, I was stumbling around, unfocused, in a daze. Lizzie mentioned my condition to our chaperone, who said, "Tell Margaret to stop giving away her dinner and eat her food."

I forced myself to eat. My light-headedness improved, but my love for Roland remained the same. We parted on day three, promising to write and to see each other in the near future.

When Daddy said I better not have a boyfriend, I felt compelled to write to him saying, "I cannot have a boyfriend."

That letter put an end to Roland, the love of my life.

I had to take my mind off Roland. I needed to do something rudimentary yet requiring mental focus. I decided to enter another civic-minded Rotary club writing contest. The topic this time was "What Does Freedom Mean to Me." That was not too difficult for me. As I was writing, I thought about Daddy and the "freedom" my sisters desired. My essay was written.

I won.

The prize this time was a $50 savings bond. I received congratulations from friends, relatives, and teachers.

Of course, I played the whole thing down, "Oh, thank you, but it's no big deal. I just wrote something—it wasn't anything."

My parents gave the same low-keyed response as they did back in seventh grade.

Mama said, "You kin use dat money fer college."

Daddy said, "You ain't gon spend dat money. We gon go to de bank an open a account so you kin deposit dat money."

Depositing the savings certificate into my very own bank account gave Daddy a chance to show me his business side.

Chapter Thirty-One

Cars, 'Wine' & A Kiss

Jean and I somehow had so much to talk about these days. Mostly we talked about Daddy and how strict he was with Mae, Leeah and Ruth.

Mae used to ask Daddy if she could go to visit her friends, Freida and Trish. She got tired of hearing him say "No." His lecture was even worse: "You ain't goin to nobody's house. You don't know nothin' 'bout dese people. All kinda men be hangin 'round dese places. You need to be studin, not runnin to nobidys house."

She stopped asking. She spent a lot of time on the telephone with her friends, talking, laughing, and practicing Spanish.

Leeah, more than Ruth, kept talking about wanting to go to parties. I asked Leeah one time, "What party do you want to go to?"

"How do I know?" she said. "There are parties all the time, but nobody invites us, 'cause they know we can't come."

Daddy felt he needed to have control of my sister's movements and their social interactions. They couldn't be with a boyfriend except in the courting room. They couldn't go to town and just walk around. They couldn't go to a friend's house. Jean was more exasperated by the situation than I was.

"How are we supposed to know how to act if we can't do anything or go anywhere? Daddy was judging us by what he would do. When we do leave home, I bet we're going to be so wild."

Daddy finally sold the truck, after Junior hit a car when he was backing out into the road. Daddy yelled at Junior and the man yelled at Junior and at Daddy. After that, Daddy bought only cars. A used green Buick was our first car. Daddy said that was "a good car, the best car we ever had." He said that after our brand new 1959 Dodge proved to be "the worst car we ever had."

That brand-new, brown and white, 1959 Dodge with fins sticking up in the back like an airplane was the best-looking car we ever had.

That car was so fancy people were driving by real slow, just to take a look at it. We were all out in the front of the house admiring that "space" car. Mrs. Fanny was there. Aunt Helen, Uncle Jay, Uncle Lester, Aunt Erma, and our cousins were there, all touching and rubbing and heaping niceties on that car. Ed and Peggy Hines were there, too, along with their girls, Carol and Kay. We were so surprised that almost all our neighbors came out into the road to see that car and stayed until late into the evening.

The next day, Uncle Lester pulled into his driveway with a new red and white 1959 Dodge with fins sticking up in the back like an airplane. When we saw that, everybody was flabbergasted. Nobody asked the question, "Why did he get a new car one day after we did?" or more importantly, "Why did he get the same car that we bought just in a different color?" The question "Are you that pathetic?" was not asked either.

Mama, and especially my older sisters, railed at the "stupidity and jealousy" of it all. We did our duty and walked down to their house and touched, rubbed, and admired the car and the color. We heaped niceties on that car until late into the evening. Aunt Helen and Uncle Jay and the other neighbors didn't come out for this showing.

We were at Uncle Lester's house to admire his new car. But Daddy had a nose for degradation. When he sensed what was going on at his brother's house, we were forbidden to go there ever again.

Uncle Lester was working as a butcher at the Freeland Farm, and Aunt Erma was working as a cleaning lady "day and night" for the owner of a tire company. Daddy determined that there was no supervision in that house whatsoever.

"Louise is wild—goin to dancing parties and all kind of peoples coming to dat house. When I wuz young, I never danced an never went to no parties—an y'all don't need to netha. I never had no beer or whiskey or played all dem games young peoples played. All dey do down dere is drank dat 7-Up. Louise wuz dranking out dere in da yard tonite."

Ruth protested, "She was drinking 7-Up. It's just soda pop!"

Daddy was adamant, "Dat ain't no soda pop! I never had no beer or whisky, but I know dranking. Dat is wine! I better not ketch none of y'all down dere no mo."

The word "ketch" is the operative word here. When Daddy was at work, the traffic from our house to see what was going on at Louise's house continued.

For the most part though, we were homebound after that. Nobody dared to ask to go anywhere.

Daddy had rules for Mama, too. He didn't want coffee or coffee drinking in the house. Mama, like my sisters, found ways to get around some of Daddy's rules. When Daddy was at work, Uncle Jay brought ready-made coffee to the house. He and Mama still sat in the dining room talking and sipping coffee from their saucers.

If by chance, somebody was allowed to go somewhere, a lecture always came first.

From Mama: "Don't be silly. Keep yo dress tail down."

From Daddy: "You don't need to go nowhere. Dese niggers in Mt. Vernon, ain't none of dem no good. Y'all oughtta be thanking 'bout something else 'cept keeping you feet in the road. Don't you ast to go nowhere else 'cause you aint goin nowhere."

One time, Jean was invited to a birthday party. I was not invited, but we all knew that if Jean was going, I was going with her. It was always like that.

It took about a week of "back and forth" between Mama, Jean, and Daddy, before we were allowed to go. It was a process, and the process was always the same. I had no interest in getting involved: "Mama can we go to Betty's birthday party?"

"Ask your Daddy."

"Daddy, can we go to Betty's birthday party?"

"You ain't going to no party."

Two days before the party: "Mama, are we going to Betty's party?"

"What did yo Daddy say?

"He said 'no.' He always says the same thing. I don't know why we always have to go through this every time we want to go somewhere."

Two hours before the seven o'clock party: "Mama are we going to the party? We've been asking all week. Why can't we just get an answer? Nobody else in the whole world has to go through the third degree just to go to a birthday party!"

"Willie T, you gon let dem go to dis party?"

"I told y'all you ain't goin to no party."

"But Willie, it's jes one party an you know Miss Ellen an Miss Bulah gon be dere. Dey kin go dere fer a lit'l while."

"Why you always goin aginst wat I say? I don't care who gon be dere—y'all should be doin something else 'cept thanking 'bout stuff dat ain't gon help you in life."

Jean interjected, "Being with other people is gonna help us in life—just staying up under y'all all the time—"

Daddy had the last word: "Y'all go over der an you be ready to come home at nine o'clock. An don't you ast to go nowhere else."

We got to the party late. Just as Jean entered the room, the music stopped. Jean saw this as an acknowledgment that she had arrived and that this was her moment. She stood in the silent light, smiling broadly, and basking in the attention of her audience. She surveyed the room with extended arms, fluttering eyelashes, and a facial expression that seemed to ask, "Y'all were waiting for me?"

I walked past her and into the next room. There was a game of Spin the Bottle going on. I had never played this game before, but I found a place on the floor between two high school boys. And before I had learned the game, the spinning bottle stopped, it's opening pointing at one of the boys next to me. I was smiling, when the "winner" grabbed me. His lips touched mine; his tongue thrust searchingly into my mouth. I was about to choke, when cold saliva oozed over my tongue. It felt like my mouth was full of buttermilk with biscuit! It felt outright nasty.

I was finally released to cheers and "woo-hoos" from the other gamers. I put on a no-teeth smile and excused myself. I rushed to the bathroom and dribbled spit into the sink.

I felt good though. Wow—my first kiss! And it didn't matter that my kisser, Bailey, was a distant cousin.

Chapter Thirty-Two

We Coulda Sang for Aretha

"Sista, you gotta bring the girls to Detroit."

That was Aunt Belle talking on the phone. Mae, Leeah, and Mama were trying to listen in, all at the same time.

"I got it all set up. I've talked to the program managers, and the Edward Sisters are on the program. It's gonna be at Aretha Franklin's church. Aretha will be there, Martha, and—"

Mama was trying to understand, "Belle, wat chu talking 'bout?—Willie ain't gon brang dese kids up dere—he can't—"

We were trying to listen, and Leeah was trying to find out what Aretha had to do with us.

"What—is she saying? We can sing with Aretha Franklin—in Detroit? I wanna go."

Aunt Belle continued to make her case. "Sista, he's got to bring them. It's all arranged. A lot of the big stars are going to be there. This is a great opportunity for the girls. They will have a chance to be heard by the best—Let me talk to T."

Daddy listened to Aunt Belle. Then we heard what he said, "I ain't gon let my kids sang fer these peoples talking about no records—dey don't sang dat kinda stuff. I know wat dese kind of peoples is lak, and I ain't gittin involved wit dese peoples. Dat ain't no place fer these chillun to be at."

He handed the phone back to Mama.

My sisters started yelling. Even Jean was joining in.

Me? I was just listening to see which way this thing was going to go.

"We can't go? All the big stars gonna be there, and we can't go? What is wrong with y'all? Why can't we go? It's already arranged—we're on the program—they want to hear us sing! Why are you always holding us back? Aunt Belle said she's gon buy the tickets!"

Aunt Belle was still begging too. "I'll buy the tickets, T. Don't embarrass me now. I worked so hard to get them on the program. I just want to get them here, Sista. You got to talk to T."

Mama asked, "Willie T, what you wont me to tell Belle? She don did a lot to git these kids on the program."

Daddy's reply was, "Tell her 'Thank you,' but dey ain't gon sang up dere. This whole thang ain't nothin but a racket."

Leeah was yelling, "You don't know what you talking about. Aunt Belle knows these people—why can't we just go and see?" Mae and Jean were yelling, "We want to go and see—Aretha sings gospel music—we can sing with her".

Daddy put on his work shoes and left, leaving Mama on the phone with Aunt Belle.

I didn't quite know how I was supposed to feel. I wasn't sure who Aretha was, but I knew of Stevie Wonder. Because Aunt Belle had arranged for us to sing, I bet there were going to be a lot of sophisticated people there.

My sisters were so mad. They tried not to be in the same room with Daddy. They just did their jobs, washed, cleaned, and whipped out flies. They did what they were told without comment. They moped round the house. Everybody was just walking around not talking or laughing or anything. I didn't like being around Daddy either.

Every word out of my sisters' mouths when they were out of Daddy's sight was focused on the same mantra, "I can't wait to get outta this house."

The feeling was that Daddy had stifled the biggest, and last, opportunity to advance our singing career. I think Mama felt that way, too.

Chapter Thirty-Three

Leaving Home Capers

People liked our singing, but there was a love–hate relationship regarding our family as a whole. Parents loved the fact that Junior was "going out with my daughter," or that Leeah was "talking to my son." Being with one of the Edwards children meant possible money and prestige.

Other families were suspicious of Daddy for having the means to buy acres of land, build a beautiful house, and do it with so many kids. We also owned two "nice" houses on 10th Street that were being rented. People were also suspicious about Daddy's NAACP work and his intentions regarding Washington School.

Even one time, Jerri asked me, "Do you think you better than us?"

She caught me off guard with that question. The answer I felt and wanted to say was "Yes," but I didn't want to get beat up, so I said, "No, of course not. Why you ask me such a question?"

There were very few young Black men of age for my sisters to go out with. Of the 1,500 students in the high school, grades nine through twelve, no more than eight were Black boys. And fewer still who were considered "eligible." That meant the boys had to excel in school, have a good job, or come from a "good family."

Even my brother Junior only met one of the eligibility criteria. He was considered to be "from a good family." He was not a good student and when he got a job, it was washing cars. Even so, he was highly sought after in high school, by what Leeah referred to as "sluts," like Alistine, and "old ugly women" like Johna Sue.

When Mama and Daddy were not home and Junior was talking on the phone to one of his "friends," he had to endure Leeah's yelling at his choices.

"You're no good. You're a nasty slut, and I don't know why Junior hangs around with you."

Junior would slap at her trying to get her to get away from the phone. She would continue grabbing and yelling, "You old black buzzard. You ain't nothin' but a stinking skunk"

He would usually just hang up the phone. He never hit or yelled at her. I always wondered why not.

Girls from "good families," like the barber shop owner's daughter, Susana, pursued Junior, but he seemed to prefer the two former types.

Daddy had to know about Junior's behavior, but he never said anything. Leeah always voiced her opinion on the subject.

"Why don't Daddy say anything to Junior about those slutty girls he fools around with? He's always talking to us about 'what men want.' I don't care what men want. What about what I want?"

Junior never went to church. In high school, he always went out with Roy and B.B., but sometimes, he stayed out all night. And yet, I never heard Daddy say anything. Daddy never talked to him about his future and never admonished him for the kind of girls he was hanging out with.

Yet, Junior felt compelled to enroll in junior college. But after a couple of months, a letter from the college arrived in the mail.

The letter indicated that Junior was not attending classes. He had therefore been dropped from the college rolls. Knowing that his truancy would come to light, Junior had signed up and enlisted in the U.S. Army. Both revelations brought a lot of weeping and wailing from Mama.

"Why, Junior? You ain't ready fer no army. You been goin ta skool everday. Why you doin dis?"

Daddy didn't say a word. I wondered what he was thinking. Maybe he was glad to have Junior leave Mt. Vernon as a remedy for his questionable choices in women. Or maybe he had not seen in Junior any adherence to the Christian faith or to the work ethic that he valued in a man. One of Daddy's favorite scriptures was: "Be watchful, stand firm in the faith, act like men, be strong." Corinthians 16:13.

Junior's failure to embrace going to college may have been in response to his own admitted shortcomings in academia. He talked about what schooling was like for him in Mississippi and in Mt. Vernon.

"You know, in Mississippi, school was school. We went to Hardiman School everyday. It was just one room made out of planks and set way back in the woods. It was hot in there in the summer and cold in the winter. The cold months were the worst. We had to crowd around that wood stove to try to keep warm.

"We went to school starting around November and stopped around March or April. The teachers—I don't know if I would call them teachers—they were just anybody who could read a little bit—no degrees or anything. Most of them were just there for a little while, and then somebody else would come.

"There were about fifteen kids in the class, but on most days, there was five or six, depending on the planting season. All different ages, five-year-olds up to about seventeen years old were in the same room. So, the teacher just told stories and gave us words to copy in a little tablet. Sometimes, we did some adding and subtracting, but I know we didn't learn much—that's just the way it was.

"Mr. Hardiman was there for a long time, and he was educated. He was the last and the best teacher we had before we left Mississippi. Every teacher we got before Mr. Hardiman just talked about Abraham Lincoln and George Washington—old stuff about what they did to help Negroes and the United States. So, for five or six years, that's all we learned about.

When I started junior high in Mt. Vernon, I didn't know nothing. I didn't know how to talk. I was teased and laughed at because of my brown shoes and short pants. It got better when I got to high school."

Junior knew his limitations. And I think Daddy knew them, too. I didn't know Junior very well, since he wasn't around much.

I remember him playing the "quick hands" game with me. He raised his hand quick like he was going to hit me but scratched his head instead. Sometimes, he made music by slapping the inside and outside of his legs to some made-up tune.

The one thing I remember him most for was his love for the music of Tony Bennett. When he was in the house, he played Tony's records and swooned to the sound of that voice. I grew to love that voice, too. When I was in fourth grade, Junior became a soldier in the U.S. Army, stationed in South Korea.

With Junior gone, Daddy could concentrate on the future schooling of Mae, Leeah, and Ruth. Sustaining college enrollment for each of them would also prove to be a goal too far.

After graduating from high school, Mae enrolled as a freshman at Southern Illinois University (SIU). The university was about an hour and a half away, at Carbondale. Her enrollment at SIU was a quiet triumph, an Edwards Sister in college!

With much pride, we drove Mae to SIU and set her up in her boarding room. I was reveling in the fun she was going to have to be away from home—without rules.

Going to college was an expectation in our house. The fact that Mae did not have a strong academic record as per her 'report card checks' was not a consideration for Daddy. He ignored the fact that she had the same schooling experiences as Junior.

For a while, Mae seemed to be doing well academically and socially. She even brought home a boyfriend named Melvin one weekend.

Daddy ignored Melvin, suggesting to Mae, "You in skool ta be sturdin, not runnin 'round wit no boys."

After the first quarter, Mae got failing grades in almost every subject. When she did not improve by the end of the semester, she had to leave SIU. In an effort to keep her in college, Daddy allowed her to enroll in a smaller, less-stimulating environment. She enrolled in the junior college in Centralia, Illinois, twenty-six miles away.

She did not do well there. The "going to college" experience was over for her. She had to come home. There was quiet disappointment in the house, and especially for Mae.

Our cousins, Roy and B.B. had graduated high school and gotten jobs at state hospitals in towns like Elgin and Joliet, up near Chicago. Most Black high school graduates had successfully found employment at state hospitals as well.

To be back home and living under Daddy's roof and his rules once again was something Mae indicated, "I ain't goin do that no more."

She decided that getting a job at a state hospital could be her route out of the house, and out of Mt. Vernon. In order for this to happen, she had to pass a state test.

I don't know where the idea came from, but it did not come from me.

Mama said to me, "Margaret, you gotta take the test for Mae."

"What test? How am I going to take a test for Mae?"

Mama tried to explain, "To git a job in the state, Mae hav ta pass a test. It would be better if you take da test fer her."

I protested. "How am I supposed to do that? Why me? I'm fifteen-years-old—why can't Jean or Ruth do it?"

All I got from Mama was, "You kin probly do da best."

I know that if Daddy had not approved of this scheme, it would not have been brought forward. He said nothing to me about the idea, and he said nothing on the drive to the testing site. He let Mama do all the talking.

I continued to voice my concern, trying not to say anything to hurt Mae's feelings. She was just sitting there real quiet like this was not about her. She said nothing to me about what I was going to do for her.

"What if they find out that I'm not Mae—what will happen to me then?"

Mama just said, "Jes keep yo head down an do wat dey say."

I was not happy about this whole thing. I was feeling like a dishonest cheat, like I did in third grade when I stole those earrings from Woolworths.

To sign in for the test, I had to enter Mae's name, birthdate, and social security number. I was ready for that. What I was not ready for, and what made my heart skip a beat was when the man said, "I have to take your fingerprints."

For years after this episode, I expected the FBI to come knocking on my door. I would have to explain why Mae and I had the same fingerprints. And when I told the truth, I would end up in jail or worse!

"Mae" passed the test and started a job in the state hospital in Elgin, Illinois.

The FBI never came calling.

After a few years in the state hospital system, Mae met and married a gentleman from the area. She made a most memorable observation on her wedding day: "Mama, this is embarrassing. Why are you pregnant again—and at my wedding?"

Leeah soon followed the state hospital route after a semester at the junior college. She took and passed the state test herself.

Her overt refusal to abide by the rules of the house was sufficient reason for Daddy to let her go, in order for her "to see what it's like to be on your own."

Like Jean said many times, "How are we suppose to know how to act if we can't go anywhere? I think we're all going to be wild when we leave home."

With so many graduates from Mt. Vernon working in state hospitals in the suburbs of Chicago, Leeah almost immediately "hooked up" with one of her "old friends" from high school. Her wedding was planned and held a few months after Mae's. In both weddings, I was a sixteen-year-old bridesmaid, smiling down the aisle, wearing the same frilly blue dress.

Ruth did enroll in college, just like Junior, Mae, and Leeah did. However, her going to classes was cut short when she met a young man at the NAACP convention in Atlanta. We all met him and liked him. He was short, yet handsome. But Daddy saw something else.

He warned Ruth, "Dat boy ain't gon mount ta nothing. What you doin talking to dat boy looking lak he ain't got a decent pair of pants ta wear?"

Ruth was not to be deterred. She married him. They lived at our house for a time. Andy was very likable, playful, and appeared to be kind and loving to Ruth.

I asked him one day, "Andy, are you always going to be this way to Ruth?"

His answer,"I am absolutely going to try."

He joined the military and together they headed off to Japan.

I was sure Daddy felt that he had done what he felt was best to save my three older sisters from "ruining our family." Now, that they were married, and he had successfully "kept their dress tails down" while under his roof, he had Jean and me to go.

Chapter Thirty-Four

A Perfect Paper & Joy Riding

Because I was in accelerated classes, I took journalism instead of English III. The class was responsible for writing and producing the school newspaper.

The paper's editors and writers were usually determined by the teacher, Mr. Olin, but could be determined by a test. For example, the test for the Copy Editor position was a sample "copy," and we had to correct it for mistakes using the proper notations and symbols.

The editor positions were the most sought after and were usually given to the students who were either popular, smart, or pretty, and always White. Those were the kinds of students who were in the Journalism class.

Vying for the editor positions were people like Kat, who was Homecoming Queen and whose father was a former high school principal. There was Bev, whose family owned the farm where my sisters and me picked strawberries to earn money during the summer, and who owned the butcher shop where Uncle Lester worked. The smartest boy in the school, Ned, was there, along with Kathleen, the prettiest girl in the school, and whose mother my mother worked for as a cleaner. There were fifteen other kids in the class with similar resumes. And then, there was me, the lone Black girl with flaws and no pedigree.

"Class. I have the Copy Editor test results. And who do you think got a perfect score? Who do you think found and corrected all the mistakes?"

Mr. Olin was a slim, boyish-looking young man in his dark, too big suit. He had deep hair loss on the right side of his forehead. He reached now to rake loose hair to ensure the coverage was in place.

"Come on, guess," he playfully implored us.

We were looking around at each other, smiling, shrugging our shoulders, and pointing at each other.

He said, "You give up? Okay, okay. It's Margaret."

There was a beat of silence. Everyone was confused and shocked. It took a minute before they found their manners and covered their disbelief by talking all over each other.

"Oh, wow. Great job, Margaret."

"How did you do that?"

"A perfect paper!"

I knew they were nervous. They had counted how many editor positions there were. There were seven, and if one went to Margaret—unthinkable!

To me, they didn't need to worry. Journalism teachers would do what they had always done.

Two days later, the Editor positions and the writers were posted on the classroom door for all to see.

I knew the pressure Mr. Olin was under. He was a first-year teacher. He assumed he had to honor the tradition of giving the leadership positions to a White student, the expected and the familiar. A Black student getting a perfect paper and deserving the Copy Editor position, but not getting it, in my mind should have made him angry. I wonder if it did? And what about our West Salem bus driver Mr. Gram and my singing ensemble sponsor, Miss Snodsmith?

Each did what was expected of them. However, none had the courage to do what was right.

Mr. Olin selected Mary Edelmond to be Copy Editor. She was my alphabetical seating buddy and had been for the last eight years. I was assigned to write features and "beat" stories.

I didn't make a fuss. Who would listen? Nobody would.

* * *

Doing what was easiest, in spite of the unfairness of it, became clear to me again when I was one of twenty students nominated for the National Honor Society. The selection committee faced with choice and ambiguity went again for safety. Sixteen White students were selected. They had their pictures taken and were celebrated.

I joined activities and programs in spite of "tradition or the injustice of it all," because I enjoyed them. I refused to deprive myself of trips, contests, and choirs, just because I was Black. White kids were involved in activities, and sports, and enjoying their school life. I was determined to do the same as much as possible, in spite of being relegated to participatory roles. Daddy's limitations were still in place, but I continued to sing in the chorus, traveling to performances and competitions around the city.

Many of my goings and comings happened in the evening or even at night. As long as I was involved in school or church-related activities that did not involve boys or parties or dances, Daddy never complained or refused to drive me there.

I participated in school plays and musicals and clubs, and I was a History and P.E. assistant. I was doing what I enjoyed. I asked myself, "Why should White kids enjoy being involve in their school's activities while Black kids watch from the sidelines?"

I also continued my involvement in Girl Scouts, meeting weekly and going on weeklong camping trips during the summer. I was a Scout "candy striper," which meant that I volunteered after school at Jefferson Memorial Hospital, where at least half of my fourteen siblings were born.

I happened to be in the emergency room one afternoon when a man screaming at the top of his lungs was brought in. I kicked into gear like everyone else, collecting supplies and rushing to the operating room. I could see the man's arm had been torn almost off, and his bones were jutting out of his remaining skin. It happened when the man had his arm hanging out his car window, when a truck sideswiped him and took most of his arm off.

Dr. Morton must have seen my face and said to me, "You shouldn't be in here."

He was right. I decided that any profession involving blood and bones was not for me.

* * *

"Okay, now type, 'Now is the time for all good men to come to the aid of their country.'—Again."

That was Miss Gray, trying to get our fingers to go even faster on these typewriters. She was our Business Education teacher, and she was dressed like I wanted to dress later in life. She was wearing a tight skirt and real high heels, and she liked walking around the room pushing her thick gray hair away from her face.

For now though, I was having trouble getting past my high mark of twenty words per minute. I needed to improve that number in order to confirm my career choice of becoming an executive secretary.

And shorthand? I was good at making symbols on the spiral pad, but I was having difficulty translating those symbols into words.

The White girls were naturals at typing forty words per minute and deciphering their symbols. Some even had part-time office jobs already. I didn't expect to get a typing job in Mt. Vernon. No Blacks had secretarial jobs. The only secretary work I did was for Daddy. He depended on me.

At this point, I knew the "look" of an executive secretary. The ones I saw on TV were all about efficiency. They wore simple, no-frill dresses, a string of white pearls, high heel pumps, and carried a steno flip pad. They talked on the phone and walked a lot, going in and out of the bosses' office, bringing papers, taking papers, and sometimes, bringing coffee. The secretarys on TV were always White. I had not seen a Black executive secretary yet.

The only jobs Black women had in Mt. Vernon were looking after White folks. They were cleaning their houses, cooking their food and caring for their children or their elderly parents. The exception was that a Black woman could teach Black kids at

Washington School. I intended to do none of these jobs. I smiled and nodded at church folks when they said to Mama, "Margaret is so smart. She gon be a teacha?"

Mama proudly proclaimed, "Yes, I hope so—if she keep on stirdying."

* * *

Jean and I were the only Edwards Sisters remaining at home. We continued to get requests to sing at different churches, so we came up with a repertoire of songs for two. Our most requested song was "Did You Stop to Pray This Morning."

I was not perfect, but if left to me, I generally followed the rules.

When Mrs. Brown asked Daddy if Jean and I could sing for the White ladies' garden club, he said we could. We had permission to check out of school at lunchtime and make our way to the venue by 2:00 p.m.

On our way off the school grounds, Jean said to me, "Reverend Nasbit is going to pick us up an take us over there."

I asked, "Why is he taking us there?"

"He wants to," Jean replied.

And there was Reverend Nasbit, parked on a side street near Dairy Queen. He was all suited up in brown, like a beaver. His round face and eyes were shielded by a brown fedora.

Jean opened the front door and slid into the front seat like she had done this before. I got in the back.

Rev. Nasbit spoke first, "Hi, how y'all doing?"

"Fine," we replied in unison.

"Y'all don't have to be at the hall until two o'clock, do you want to ride around first?" Rev. Nasbit asked.

I didn't know what was going on, and I had some questions, but I kept quiet.

"Yeah, let's just go around somewhere," Jean replied.

"Okay."

Reverend Nasbit started the car and drove a block to Dairy Queen. He ordered three burgers, chicken nuggets, and three milkshakes.

"What kind of shakes you like? Vanilla okay?"

I had lots of other questions, and they had nothing to do with flavors of milkshakes.

I just let Jean do the talking. She seemed very comfortable and relaxed being in the front seat with the Reverend.

"Yeah, we like vanilla."

With the burgers and chicken bagged for later, we headed toward the White side of town, each of us sucking quietly on our milkshakes through plastic straws. For about thirty minutes, we were just driving down streets with white houses and occasionally down the highway to get to more neighborhoods with white houses.

"Y'all want to eat something? I'll just stop over here."

He pulled off the road and handed out the burgers. He propped up the chicken nuggets on the armrest for us to share.

I took the lid off my burger and smothered the thin patty with ketchup. Dairy Queen sure could make good food, and this chicken tasted nothing like the ones that ran around in our back yard. I was feeling relaxed, the food was good, but I was not happy with this situation.

"What time is it?" I asked.

Jean kept eating. Rev. Nasbit looked at his watch.

"It's 1:50."

"Should we go now?" I asked.

Jean replied, "I don't think we can get there in time—we'll be too late. Let's just not go."

I was nonplussed. We had to go, we promised. I was getting angry.

"So, what do we tell Mrs. Brown? She is expecting us to come," I said.

No one answered me. Jean and the Reverend kept chewing.

I blamed Daddy for forcing Jean to find a way to break the rules and "go somewhere." And I blamed Jean for dragging me into her rule-breaking plan.

Mrs. Brown confronted us on Sunday: "The ladies were expecting y'all to come and sing. Where were you? Why didn't you come?"

I had no answer. Jean mumbled something about having a test. I was grateful that Daddy never found out that we failed to show up at that garden party. And I am even more grateful that he never found out that we were hanging out with the Reverend!

Chapter Thirty-Five

Talking History & Seeing Change

By the early 1960s, so many things had changed in Mt. Vernon. For one thing, we didn't know very many people in town anymore, and a lot of them didn't know us. Most of the church families we had known for years were no longer around, and their children were no longer in town. Other families who had no ties to the community had replaced those families.

Mt. Vernon was the County Seat, and the city started providing financial support to families in need. That word must have gotten out around the state because families from Chicago especially flooded the town, looking for financial aid and housing. To accommodate the new arrivals, the city replaced some houses in the Black neighborhood with two-story housing projects. Most of these new people didn't integrate well into the community. Their children attended school, but the families did not attend the numerous churches in their area. They remained "outsiders."

Jean graduated from high school in the middle of this new

environment. And as expected, she enrolled in the junior college.

Nothing changed for us. Jean still hung around with me in the high school courtyard. No other Black kids were enrolled in college. She was marking time. That was not what I intended to do.

* * *

My senior year and 1963 started out with great promise. I was again in accelerated classes, and my favorites were History and English. I loved studying the Civil War and learning about the bravery of our great generals. I could name each general and the battles they won or lost. I guessed there weren't any Colored soldiers in the war, because I didn't hear or read anything about them.

I could recite the Preamble, the Declaration of Independence, and the Gettysburg Address. I could recite Shakespeare's famous soliloquy from MacBeth, "Tomorrow, and tomorrow and tomorrow."

I learned about WWI and WWII, about German and Japanese hegemony, and about autocrats and dictators. My notebook was filled with outlines of each chapter in the history book. And I made "A's" on every test or quiz.

Jean and I related history to our current lives.

"Would you say that Daddy is a dictator?" I asked Jean.

"Of course, he is. He tells us what to do about everything, except what we wear and what we eat. All the kids I graduated with have left Mt. Vernon, or at least they can drive their car and go anywhere they want to. Nobody in this house can drive, except Daddy."

"Yep," I said. "That is what dictators do. They keep you depending on them for everything."

It was in my History class that I met two White girls, Janice and Sylvia, who became my good friends. I already knew them, but having most of our classes together illuminated just how much we had in common.

We each had our flaws. Sylvia was homely and overweight with stringy brown hair. Janice was shy, as she attempted to disguise a limp. I hid in classes, refusing to raise my hand and call attention to my acne.

We were alike—quiet, smart, and a little bit country. We talked about feeding pigs, hoeing grass, and picking berries. They lost me though when they started talking about boyfriends, pickup trucks, and Dolly Parton.

We mostly conferred on writing assignments and marveled at how Robert Frost's poem "The Road Less Traveled By" related to our lives.

We listened to each other's possible phraseology and topic sentences for writing assignments. We met and talked at lunch in the library. We enjoyed each other's company immensely.

Then our world shattered with the assassination of President Kennedy. He and his family were so young. Never before had I seen high school students and teachers dissolve into such outward displays of grief and sorrow. It became even more important then for me to focus on my future and my career.

* * *

The one thing that changed during my high school years that I had not focused on was 28th Street. Little Moe and Miss Tiny passed away. The McDonald family moved away, as did the Hines family. All three houses were demolished.

Louise left and joined her older brothers up near Chicago. Gilbert got married, left his family behind, and went to Kentucky to work in the mines. "Fatty" and "Skinny" Tarnes finally moved to Chicago to be with their son, Alfie.

The number of families on 28th Street shrunk to three except for random renters showing up and parking a trailer in an empty field.

Big Papa died. Miss Mary found him in the cornfield between our house and 29th Street. That's the first time I saw Daddy shed a tear.

Chapter Thirty-Six

The Prom

I did go to the prom, but I had to be talked into going. I had learned my lesson from Jean's ordeal the year before.

She made the mistake of asking Daddy if she could go. And because of that, she had to go through the "you ain't going nowhere" process. And when she finally did get to go, she had to be home in two hours.

She recounted the humiliating experience:

"I could not believe I had to be home so early. Will was teasing me. Everybody was laughing at me; they couldn't believe it. And when I got home, Daddy was waiting for me. He made me get up at six o'clock in the morning. I had to go out and chop weeds in the garden. Just me—nobody else—and just because I went to the prom for two hours."

After hearing that, I decided not to ask to go to the prom. Mainly because there were no boys to go with and the word "boring" was the description used by those who had gone.

I decided that, for the sake of peace, I would avoid bringing up the subject. One thing I became known for during the final months of my senior year in high school was to start acting my age. I was about to graduate. I told myself that I would no longer follow every directive my parents handed down. In any case, I decided to wait to be asked if I wanted to go.

Jean did the honors at supper one evening a few days before the prom. "Margaret, are you going to the prom?"

"Probably not," I answered. "It's too much trouble, and I don't have anyone to go with. Bobby asked me, but—you know how that is. I don't want to go with him."

Daddy said nothing; Mama said nothing. I knew they were listening.

Jean continued, "Bobby? You don't have to worry 'bout him. You might as well go by yourself. But I like Bobby."

Mama asked, "When is the prom?"

I answered, "Friday night."

When Daddy had nothing to say when the words "going" and "boy" were in the same sentence, I knew I could go.

Jean was befuddled. "What is happening? Daddy didn't say nothing about you going to the prom?"

I just said, "I know how to play the game now. I have broken the code."

So, Jean brought out the blue bridesmaid dress I wore for both of my sisters' weddings. It was not fancy, like the long dresses in the windows at Gladstone's, with lace and hooped skirts. My ankle-length dress was sleeveless with blue ruffles along the hemline.

While Daddy was in town buying groceries, Jean and I went to Jannie's Flower Shop to pick out a boutonniere for Bobby.

The place was packed with White classmates and their mothers's all "oohing" and "aahing" and chatting loudly about dresses, boutonnieres, and corsages.

My friend, Kathleen, and her mother saw me, and I saw them. Mama still worked as a house cleaner for them. I hoped I was not wearing one of Kathleen's hand-me-down dresses.

"Hi Margaret."

Kathleen was speaking to me across a counter. Her mother waved to me and went to the cashier to collect the boutonniere that I was sure she ordered two weeks ago. Kathleen was flashing her glossy white teeth and throwing her blonde curls from side to side.

"Isn't this exciting!"

I thought, *Of course, it's exciting for you. You're White and you're in the running for Prom Queen!*

"Did you go last year?"

"No," I said. "My first time."

"Oh, you're gonna have so much fun. Who're you going with, Toney King? He is so nice."

"No, I'm not going with Toney. I'm going with Bobby."

White people always like the one Colored guy who can play sports, and think other Black people should like that guy, too. They don't know Toney's family or his backstory.

The Toney Kathleen calls "so nice" is the 'sports darling' of the White kids and the White teachers because he is the 'star' of the high school's winning basketball and football teams. He is never seen with Black kids at school and Whites don't know the torment that Toney probably feels everyday because he works so hard to be accepted by Whites. And they don't know that because of his hard work, he would never ask me, a Black girl, to go with him to the prom. And they don't know that because Daddy knows the family's story, I would not be allowed to go to the prom with him anyway.

Kathleen was still looking at flowers and talking, "Oh," she said with surprise in her blue eyes. "I don't know Bobby. But I'm sure he is a great guy like Toney—Well, I've gotta go pick up my dress—but I'll see you tonight." She gave me an exit wave. "Bye."

"See you."

I settled on a leftover simple white flower boutonniere for Bobby.

* * *

Aunt Helen pressed and "flipped" my hair just below my shoulders for two dollars. My face was powdered, my cheeks had a hint of red rouge, and my lips were red to match. I looked pretty, and I felt too pretty to be going to a prom, and especially with the guy who happened to be the only one available and acceptable to Daddy.

When Bobby came to the house to pick me up, he arrived wearing that same dark blue suit he wore to church and he was carrying a small white box.

At least we are both in blue, I thought.

Sometimes in certain situations, I allow myself to have an "out of body" experience. I had one of those experiences now with Bobby. Jean took over, while my little sisters and brothers and Mama stood and watched from different doorways. They all were more excited than I was. Plus, this was entertaining. No boy had come to the house all dressed up to go out and do so in an atmosphere of good cheer and joy.

Jean handed me the boutonniere. I pinned it on Bobby's left

lapel. It fell off and rolled across the floor. Snickering erupted all around. Jean scurried to collect it. The second try was a success. When Bobby put the corsage of white flowers on my wrist, it was successful the first time.

As we were walking out the front door, followed by a trail of little sisters and brothers, Daddy appeared from a doorway to tell Bobby, "Don't keep Margaret out too late."

When we got in the car, Bobby asked me, "What time do you have to be home?"

I said, "When it's over."

We arrived at the gym, which had been transformed by red, white, and blue streamers hanging from the ceiling, covering the walls, and draping over a raised center stage. We found the other Black attendees, Rosilee and Essie, standing along a wall. They had no dates. They were dressed in their church clothes.

"Why aren't you all dancing?" I asked.

"You crazy? How we suppose to dance to this White people music!"

So, we walked around and got our pictures taken in the booth surrounded by more streamers. We visited the food tables and selected chips and fruit punch. We three girls spent a lot of time in the bathroom.

Bobby didn't know how to dance, and I didn't either. I never got to practice during American Bandstand 'cause I always had to be the "lookout." Plus, dancing was against the rules.

The evening included my friend, Kathleen, being crowned "Queen."

After a lot of screaming Kathleen, with tears in her eyes and her arms splayed toward her audience, was saying, "I can't believe I won." The losing would-be queens comforted her with, "You deserved it," and "Don't cry, we are so happy for you."

Kathleen's White boyfriend, Burt was crowned "King." He was surrounded by the losing kings, and by his sports buddies all shaking his hands, offering playful jabs and lots of "woo-hoos". I expected to see Toney among the revelers. He was absent. I guess he couldn't get a date for the prom.

We all walked down the street to the Rotary club for breakfast. I had cold pancakes, sausage, and orange juice.

I got home around five o'clock in the morning. Mama opened the door for me, and I went to bed.

Chapter Thirty-Seven

Crossing the Stage & Junior College

My graduation from high school was the sixth one for my parents. And with most events that happened in my school life, they did not let this event take on undue importance. For them, they were obliged to use the two tickets to come see me walk across the stage and be handed a diploma.

It was the month before graduation that was the most exciting for me.

The high school counselor, Mr. Sheath was in charge of getting us ready for our future. He was a big man, always wearing a grey tweed jacket. He had a cleft lip, which he tried unsuccessfully to hide under a thick brown mustache. Everybody liked him because he was just a 'regular' person. Plus, his house was across the street from our church, Pavey Chapel. We said "Hi" to him on Sundays if he was in his front yard.

He took seniors out of History classes and began having large group meetings in the library to talk about exam week and to schedule graduation rehearsals. Other times, we met to get information about possible career choices after high school. Those of us interested in going to college needed to see him about applications and about the ACT tests. I took notes on everything, just like I did when studying for a test. I looked around at my classmates to try to read their interest in these information sessions. Most of the boys were resting their heads on their desks or doodling with their ballpoint pens. The girls were either staring off, checking their makeup, or passing notes. I don't think most of the kids in these meetings were planning to go to college.

There was so much to learn about college applications and registering for tests. Every lunch hour, I was in Mr. Sheath's office talking about my application and getting registered for the ACT test. I had no time to worry about what the other Black kids were doing or saying; I was planning the next phase of my life, which included going to college.

I asked Jerri, "What are you going to do after graduation?"

She answered, "I'm getting outta this lame town, probably going to D.C. and get me a job."

After a week of final exams, intermixed with graduation rehearsals, graduation day arrived.

I decided to wear my fitted burgundy dress and matching clip-on earrings. On my feet were my black patent leather pumps. Aunt Helen had given me her two dollar press and curl.

I was ready to go to my graduation and so was Daddy. But that did not keep Mama from needing more time to get ready. It was always the same these days, pacing while waiting for Mama to get ready.

"Mama, come on. I'm gonna be late."

Daddy joined in, "Cora Mae, you had all day to git yo clothes ready. Colored folks is late fer everything."

We arrived at the school with twenty-five minutes to spare before the seven o'clock check-in time. Mama and Daddy were to make their way to the gym to join the other parents in the bleachers. If we did not find each other during the graduation reception, the plan was always to check near the trophy case.

I had to run to the assembly room. Among the excited chatter, I located and slipped on my black robe, collected my cap and orange tassel, and got in line, ready to march through the gym to the sound of the high school band playing "Pomp and Circumstance."

As usual, we marched in alphabetically, and I sat next to Mary Edelmon as I had done since West Salem.

"Hi again," she said. "This may be the last time we sit together." She pretended to cry.

I smiled, "Who knows? We may just run into each other again, somewhere."

During the ceremony, we heard the principal talk about "going out into the world to do good" and encouraging us to follow our passion. I tried hard to listen for how these words applied to my future. I couldn't make a connection right then.

We then rose in turn to cross the stage to collect our diplomas. With the calling of some graduates' names, several parents yelled and clapped their approval; with others, seemingly no parent claps were heard. Then I heard my name, "Margaret A. Edwards, graduates with Honors." I was smiling big and walking strong to shake hands with handsome Mr. Kane, who handed me my diploma and my honors certificate. I don't remember hearing cheers, but I know they were there.

The evening was bittersweet. During the reception and between fruit punch, cookies, and cheese-salad sandwiches, there were lots of hugs, tears, and "good lucks" among the class of three hundred students. I sought out as many of my West Salem friends as possible. We knew we would see each other, but never hang out with each other. We occupied different circles. Most of them would stay in town, get jobs, and get married.

For the ten graduating Black students, we exchanged "good lucks" as well, knowing we would see each other again in the next few weeks and on and off in some distant future. There were no "desk jobs" for any of them in Mt. Vernon. Most would leave looking for jobs in St. Louis, California, or Washington D.C.

Like it was for Jean and all of us, Daddy had decided that I was going to junior college, which was across the street from the high school. That was his decision regarding my immediate future. Jean would finish two years of junior college, I would finish one year, and we both then would transfer together to Southern Illinois University. It was an agreeable plan. My high school grades qualified me to receive a tuition scholarship, which I planned to use at SIU.

Graduating from high school brought relatively little change to my life. I went home to my same middle bedroom that I shared with Jean. Clothes had to be washed and ironed, the house had to be cleaned, and dishes washed and dried.

In high school, we were bus riders. Jean and I were no longer high schoolers; we just continued to ride with our younger siblings. So, we spent the year catching the 7:30 a.m. bus on the corner of 28th Street and Fishers Lane and returning home on the 4:00 p.m. bus.

We still got in the car with Daddy every Sunday and went to church. The congregation was smaller and older now. Jean was called on more often to play the piano in the absence of Mrs. Hart. I kept going to church because I had always gone, and there was nowhere else to go. Visiting singing groups from Chicago or St. Louis were no longer being invited to perform. There was not enough congregation or churchgoers to support these groups. Jean and I were still occasionally called on to sing at a church program. We were the oldest young people attending our church, so my "girlfriends" at church, Lizzie and Kate, were a year behind me.

Mr. Henderson passed away, and Big Mama was still making cakes. I had less of a sweet tooth these days but going to visit her was still a Sunday outing.

I didn't know what college was supposed to feel like. But attending Mt. Vernon Junior College made me feel like I was still in high school. Enrollment at the college was quite small. My required classes had five or six students. After a few days of seeing the same faces in classes, and in the student lounge, I had to conclude that only about twenty students were enrolled. All were White, except Jean and me.

The core college teachers and the high school teachers were the same. I knew them; they knew me. The classes were in different rooms, but in the same buildings. As a first-year college student, I was required to take History, English, Math, and a foreign language. Jean and I took French.

We took French because that was the only foreign language

offered. I learned right away that starting to learn a new language at eighteen was an almost impossible task. They hired a petite, young French woman named Miss Martin, who was trying so hard to teach the five of us in the class how to twist our lips around impossible phrases. She always had a confounded look on her face when her pronunciation of a basic phrase like "Comment allez-vous" came out of our mouths as "Come o talli voos."

None of us learned much French, but she was so likable, and so determined.

When I graduated from high school, I didn't expect my social life to improve, and it didn't. My friend Steve and his cousin Will graduated with Jean and left town. The three boys who graduated with me left town as well. Jean and I were the only Black girls our age in town.

I continued to look to the future to bring change to my life. For the time being, I accepted the situation for what it was. I spent my breaks between classes walking into town, eating cheese and peanut butter sandwiches in the lounge, and practicing and slaughtering the French language. Mostly though, I spent time hanging outside at a picnic table in the high school yard, studying with Janice and Sylvia.

One time near the end of our year, we decided to meet on Saturday in the park to talk and to contemplate our futures. Saturdays at our house continued to be the day to get ready for Sunday. This cloudy, hot day, I left the chores to my remaining ten siblings and joined my friends in the park at the swings.

I weighed about 105 pounds. It's what I weighed since junior high school. For all that time, my red shorts with my white blouse had been my casual "go to" outfit. I was wearing my shorts and blouse that day. I was a bit annoyed at myself, though, for thinking about what to wear to meet two girls I saw and talked to every day at school. I knew they were not thinking about silly stuff like, "What should I wear to the park?"

But I knew where my discomfort was coming from. It was coming from this made-up reason to meet. I knew why we got together at school, to talk about WWI and Shakespeare. In the park, we had to create a conversation about our futures, when I knew the playing field was unequal.

When I got to the park, Janice and Sylvia were already there, sitting on the swings, dragging their feet through the dirt. They were both wearing pedal pushers.

We decided to walk around, though there was not much to see. We ended up buying snow cones and eating at a picnic table. I chose the cherry, and Sylvia and Janice went for the strawberry flavor.

"What are you going to do, Janice, now that we are free?" I asked.

"Probably go to college in Du Quoin. But after I work and make some money first."

"What are you going to major in, if you go?" I wanted to know.

"Probably elementary school teaching."

I shared my dilemma. "You know, I like History and French—but I want to do something different, like, sometimes—I think about traveling the world. Maybe I could work for the United Nations. Sometimes, I think I want to be an executive Secretary and wear fancy clothes. It's all so crazy, I know. I just want some excitement."

Sylvia put it all together. "So maybe you can do all of these things. Be a secretary first and make some money, then go to college and get a degree in History and French, and then join the UN! That would really be an exciting life."

"You know what," I said, "You will never be a counselor. By the time I do all that, I'll be about sixty years old!

"What about you, Sylvia? Don't say you want to be a counselor."

"No, no. I'm really a country girl. I don't ever want to leave home. J.R. wants to get married, but I'm not ready for that yet. So, I'll probably get a job for a while—somewhere. I think I'm finished with school for a while."

I found myself envying them. They had no plan for their future, just possibilities. And I saw no concern on their faces. They had the freedom to be free of concern. I did not have the luxury of choosing to work or not or going to college or not.

I said, "Well, for sure, I'm going to SIU in September, and if I need money, I'm gonna have to get a loan."

I didn't get any clarity about what career I would pursue at SIU. I was left with questions to ponder.

We parted with hugs, hoping to see each other again.

Chapter Thirty-Eight

The Pink and Green Room

The only person we knew who was having a successful academic experience at SIU was Alton, Leeah's Lover's Lane boyfriend from high school. We knew he was at SIU, because we saw him a few times in Mt. Vernon when he was visiting his parents. Daddy decided to ask him for help in securing off campus housing for Jean and me. We could never afford to live in a dorm, and according to Alton, most Black students lived off campus in trailers or student apartments.

Daddy made it clear to Alton that he wanted us to live in a house, preferably with a single, older Christian woman. Within a week, we were provided with a name, address, and a phone number of a woman who he said, "You will like her." We just needed to make a time to visit before September. Mama, Daddy, Jean, and I arranged for a Saturday visit in August.

Daddy was somewhat familiar with Carbondale, since Mae's time here more than five years ago. So, when we turned into what was the Black side of town, I paid attention. The area looked much like Big Mama's neighborhood. Lots of old, wood-frame houses with porches and small patches of green in the front intermixed with trailers alongside newly built longhouses. Three Black boys were kicking a ball in the street and moved to the side as we passed. We stopped in front of a house like the other ones in the neighborhood. This one had a swing hanging from chains on the porch. An older woman in a pressed housedress and graying hair in a bun was standing on the porch. She appeared to be unsteady on her feet. A smiling, energetic, dark-skinned young woman rushed to meet us in the yard.

"Hi, hi. Come on in." She shook everybody's hand enthusiastically.

"I'm Mary, and this is my mother, Mrs. Hathaway." We went through another round of handshakes.

Mary was still talking and waving her arms. "This is her house. I'm here to show you around. I grew up in this house when my mother died, and my father married Mama Hathaway, and she raised seven of us—"

I was looking down the street, trying to see what else and who else may live on this street. There was a trailer across the street on the corner, and apartments were just around the corner. So, we wouldn't be isolated.

We walked down a short walkway, up onto the porch and into the living room. There was light and the floor creaked beneath our feet. I saw a church fan laying on the coffee table. We passed through as Mary continued to guide us.

"Mama's bedroom is over here," she pointed to a door. She walked to the other side of the living room. "And your bedroom is in here."

She opened the door to a room covered with pink and green flowered wallpaper and twin beds on each side. In front of the one window was a white chest of drawers—two for Jean and two for me. A small lamp sat on each corner of the chest. In front of each bed was a small, multicolored rug.

The beds were small, more like cots. They were covered with matching yellow and green quilts. A green blanket was rolled up at the foot of each bed. On the right side of the room was a small open closet with hangers. Enough room for our hanging clothes, I guessed the suitcase could go under a bed.

I tried to imagine living in this room. It smelled like mothballs, but I guess that's because no one had slept here for a while.

Opening the window would help with the smell and pulling up the shade should help get more light in here, too.

I walked over to take a look out the window. The floor squeaked with each step. Not good floors for sneaking in or out after hours.

The tour continued. "Back here is the kitchen. You can use the stove, and you have a shelf in the refrigerator for anything you need to keep cold. There are no really strict rules, just ask for what you want. The bathroom—"

I was watching Mama Hathaway. I wanted to hear from her. This was her house and her rules. I wanted to make sure that her house was not going to be like living at home. But she was not revealing much. She was just following along with our group, listening. Because she raised seven kids, she might be inclined to treat Jean and me like we were her kids.

So, I asked her a question, "Mrs. Hathaway, does the university require that you follow their rules—I mean, things like the eleven o'clock curfew?"

She seemed to be caught off-guard by the question. "The university don't tell me nothing. I hope y'all don't be coming in at all times a night. I'm a Christian woman, and Mary knows I knows something 'bout boys an girls. A lot of frolicking ain't good for you if you trying to do good in school."

Daddy added his support, "Dat's what they gon be here fer, to stirdy. Not being in de street."

Daddy was sold on Mrs. Hathaway. I had my doubts.

When we left, we followed the path that we would use to walk to campus. Once out of the neighborhood, it was a short five or six blocks.

Mama asked, "How y'all lak the place?"

I let Jean answer. "It's okay. I don't know if I'm gonna like living in somebody else's house. But Mary is nice."

Two weeks later, on a Sunday, Daddy dropped us off at Mrs. Hathaway's house. During the week before, I was quietly preparing for that day. I didn't want Daddy, especially, to see my excitement or eagerness to leave home. My preparations were done when he was at work. I got my hair done, applied my acne medication to my face more strategically, and gathered up underclothes, stockings, and hair products. I ironed my best dresses, skirts, and blouses and put them in a hanging clothes bag. We decided to take one suitcase for bulky stuff.

Chapter Thirty-Nine

My Turn

When I got out of the car and walked into that pink and green room that I was to share with Jean for the next two years, I was excited and hopeful. The room smelled clean and airy. The window was open, and the lights were on. I hung my clothing bag in the closet. Jean was humming and emptying the suitcase. I squeaked my way out to the porch. It was a warm, breezy September day.

I sat on the swing and pushed myself gently back and forth, not thinking about myself. I was thinking about my sisters, all my siblings still at home, and about my good fortune to have survived Daddy's "boot camp."

I watched a few kids coming down the block in a rusty, beat-up, red wagon. They were yelling, laughing, and spilling out, and getting up and into the wagon again. I did that once. They spilled out in front of where I was sitting. There were three of them, two girls and a boy. The girls had their hair in three braids. Maybe they had just come from church and were now wearing their play clothes.

One girl was no more than four, and the other two were seven or eight years old. When they spilled, I smiled to myself. That was like my sisters and me out there. The two older kids got in the wagon. The little one picked up the wagon handle and began to pull.

"They're too heavy for her," I said to myself. But it must be her turn. She was pulling and pulling, and the riders were hitting the sides of the wagon to urge her on. I laughed, a bit too loud. She looked in my direction. I waved. She threw up one hand, stared at me, then turned her back and slowly continued her effort to move that wagon down the street. I rose up from the swing and peered after her as she pulled and pulled and slowly moved that wagon down the street and out of sight. I waved and waved again, as I murmured, "Good-bye."

Acknowledgments

Thank you to my children, their families and my grandchildren who have given me a deep appreciation of what enduring family bonds mean.

To my husband who always believed in me and my story.

To my extended family, friends and community for providing the environment that helped me discover that I had a story to tell.

About the Author

Margaret Edwards attended Southern Illinois University (SIU), Columbia University, and Harvard University. She received a Ph.D. from The American University in Washington, DC, and spent 30 years working abroad in International Education. She is the mother of two children. She lives in Florida with her husband.

Email the author at: mar01gar04@gmail.com

Made in the USA
Las Vegas, NV
20 September 2023